T0289129

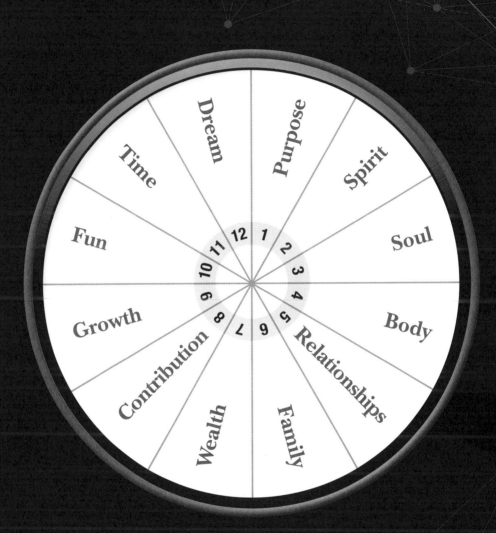

And so, dear brothers and sisters, I plead with you to give your bodies to God because of all he has done for you. Let them be a living and holy sacrifice—the kind he will find acceptable. This is truly the way to worship him. Don't copy the behavior and customs of this world, but let God transform you into a new person by changing the way you think. Then you will learn to know God's will for you, which is good and pleasing and perfect.

Because of the privilege and authority God has given me, I give each of you this warning: Don't think you are better than you really are. Be honest in your evaluation of yourselves, measuring yourselves by the faith God has given us. Just as our bodies have many parts and each part has a special function, so it is with Christ's body. We are many parts of one body, and we all belong to each other.

In his grace, God has given us different gifts for doing certain things well. So if God has given you the ability to prophesy, speak out with as much faith as God has given you. If your gift is serving others, serve them well. If you are a teacher, teach well. If your gift is to encourage others, be encouraging. If it is giving, give generously. If God has given you leadership ability, take the responsibility seriously. And if you have a gift for showing kindness to others, do it gladly.

Don't just pretend to love others. Really love them. Hate what is wrong. Hold tightly to what is good. Love each other with genuine affection, and take delight in honoring each other. Never be lazy, but work hard and serve the Lord enthusiastically. Rejoice in our confident hope. Be patient in trouble, and keep on praying. When God's people are in need, be ready to help them. Always be eager to practice hospitality.

Bless those who persecute you. Don't curse them; pray that God will bless them. Be happy with those who are happy, and weep with those who weep. Live in harmony with each other. Don't be too proud to enjoy the company of ordinary people. And don't think you know it all!

Never pay back evil with more evil. Do things in such a way that everyone can see you are honorable. Do all that you can to live in peace with everyone.

Dear friends, never take revenge. Leave that to the righteous anger of God. For the Scriptures say,

"I will take revenge;
    I will pay them back,"
    says the Lord.
Instead, "If your enemies are hungry, feed them.
    If they are thirsty, give them something to drink.
In doing this, you will heap
    burning coals of shame on their heads."
Don't let evil conquer you, but conquer evil by doing good.

—ROMANS 12 (NLT)

I love books that have a component of the autobiographical in them, which *The Journey of a Kingsman* obviously has. In fact, it's my favorite type of read for two reasons: it not only fulfills the biblical mandate to share our testimony with the world; it also gives practical examples of how we can implement life-changing principles into our own lives. Diogo has carefully woven his testimony throughout the pages of *The Kingsman*, not only adding color and content to the fabric of his life story, but bringing us, the readers, into a new awareness of God's design for our own lives. I recommend it without hesitation.

Larry Titus
President, Kingdom Global Ministries
Colleyville, Texas

Throughout my life, I've had my share of failures and setbacks. So have you. The key to being a winner is not that you never fail, that you never get knocked down, but whether you decide to get back up at least one more time than you get knocked down.

Coach Lou Holtz
Coach, Commentator, Author, and Speaker
Orlando, Florida

When a man comes to Christ, most times, his entire family comes to Christ. When a man learns how to make the best decisions, his family will also feel the impact along life's journey. I challenge you to read *The Journey of a Kingsman* by Diogo Esteves. You will learn how to be the man, the husband, and the dad the Lord has destined you to be and to become. Your marriage will be sweeter, and your children will grow up to be wise servants of the Lord!

Rev. Samuel Rodriguez
President, National Hispanic Christian Leaders Conference
Sacramento, California

I recommend a God-sent book that can change your life. It is called *The Journey of a Kingsman* by Diogo Esteves. When we read the Scriptures, we see a lot of pictures of what our life in Christ is. One of the greatest images is that "life is a journey." We are journeying through time and life, striving to become all Christ wants us to be. As you go through the ups and downs on this journey, *The Journey of a Kingsman* will provide you what you need for success in life.

Dr. Kenneth Ulmer
Senior Pastor, Faithful Central Bible Church
Los Angeles, California

There are times we come to road signs that state "The bridge is out" or "Construction ahead." Yet, due to being distracted in life, we drive right ahead. *The Journey of a Kingsman* by Diogo Esteves is a story about a great man who became distracted by the wrong things. I encourage you to get this remarkable book, especially young men, who are beginning or taking long journeys in life. This powerful road map will help men put in place the strategies necessary for a successful journey instead of ending up where the road is out.

Dr. Glenn Burris
President, Foursquare Church
Los Angeles, California

I am sure you will be enriched and encouraged through *The Journey of a Kingsman* by Diogo Esteves. This life-changing resource will be both inspirational and instructional as you develop your life's journey for the years ahead.

Dr. David Sobrepeña
Founder, Word of Hope Church
Manila, Philippines

The Journey of a Kingsman is a story about a great young man who tried to get to the top of the life's mountain the "worldly way." In this midst of this struggle, Diogo Esteves found Christ. As a result of the lessons he learned, Diogo has written an amazing book, showing us how to make it to the top of the mountain with Christ being our daily compass.

Dr. Elmer Towns
Cofounder and Vice President, Liberty University
Lynchburg, Virginia

Diogo has viewed life from the highest mountaintops and from the lowest valleys. His life experiences have fortified him, and now us, with valuable advice for securing stable footing in our financial, familial, and spiritual lives.

Libbye Morris
Writer
Albuquerque, New Mexico

The Journey of a Kingsman by Diogo Esteves reveals God's plan for your life. Each generation is filled with men who miss the mark and live from failure to failure. I am convinced this lively and Spirit-filled book will help you not to make the mistakes that countless other men have made in their lives. This book shows how to turn "wrongs" into "rights" for now and the years to come.

Dr. David Mohan
General Superintendent Assemblies of God, New Life Assembly
Chennai, India

I've been so blessed for the opportunity to share a great friendship with Diogo in the past five months. In our weekly meetings and conversations, I have learned important, life-changing principles behind *The Journey of a Kingsman* that helped me figure out my passions, my purpose, and, above all, my true connection with God. I'm sure this book is going to touch many people around the world! God bless you all!

Danilo Brizola
Founder, Snowman Labs
Curitiba, Brazil

Every man has to learn how to turn setbacks into comebacks. Sooner or later, each man will face the daunting task of discovering the success keys to unlocking life's doors into a world of fresh and vibrant opportunities. Diogo Esteves hands us the success keys in *The Journey of a Kingsman.* I encourage you to purchase your copy, along with extra copies for fellow servants who are on life's journey with you!

Dr. James O. Davis
Founder and President, Global Church Network
Orlando, Florida

This book is an amazing journey of someone who has, over time and trials, finally found his life's purpose and is now on a mission to help others find theirs as well. Reading this book has allowed me to better understand who my Creator is, who He says I am, and why He created me. And as I begin the process of reaching my full potential, I now get a chance to live my life aware of the fact that I have a special assignment in this world, which is allowing me to change daily, for the better.

Marcia Romero
Founder, People Who Make a Difference
Orlando, Florida

After struggling with depression and adversity, Diogo Esteves was capable of reinventing himself and putting into words the necessary steps for a life of success and fulfillment. In *The Journey of a Kingsman*, he presents a godly worldview worthy of your attention and leading to self-discovery. I strongly recommend this book to men searching for meaning, or struggling with everyday life, or even for those who do not see the light at the end of the tunnel to guidance and encouragement. Through this read, one shall surely be enlightened.

Silvio Esteves
Professor
Montreal, Canada

I have known Diogo for a few years; he's definitely a changed man. *The Journey of a Kingsman* is a must-read. Very inspiring!

Leo Silva
Owner, Silva's Painting
Orlando, Florida

Being able to see a man have a genuine encounter with Christ is always an incredible experience. It also fills my heart with joy because I get the opportunity to see someone I have known since birth have his life completely turned around by God's grace.

In John 8:12, Jesus said: "I am the light of the world. If you follow me, you won't have to walk in darkness, because you will have the light that leads to life." And although our lives are full of decisions that must be carefully made, following Christ is by far the most important one of all.

My wish is that this book will be only the first of many still to come. May it reach multiple generations and bring about a drastic positive impact for years to come.

Marcia Rangel
Speech Therapist
Marlborough, Massachusetts

Diogo Esteves is a brilliant young man, charming and very talented. I know him and his family very well, and he is the real deal, open and authentic. Unlike many others, he leverages his experiences, both bad and good, to propel him forward—not toward selfish ambition but toward fulfilling God's plan for his life and for those around him. This book is a must-read for those who are ready to discover "What's next?"—those who are ready to embrace their true identities and God-given destinies, ready to live life with purpose and to the fullest. Don't lose time. Read it, and then act on it!

Paul Allen
Real Estate Investor and Pastor
Southlake, Texas

The Journey of a Kingsman is an honest, detailed account of a long ordeal conquered by the love and faithfulness of God our savior. If the art of living is the ability to use misfortune in a constructive fashion, this book has certainly achieved its purpose. Life can bring us painful moments that will forever mark us; however, such painful moments can lead us to find our true purpose in life.

Desiree Paz
Transaction Coordinator, Seven Realty
Orlando, Florida

This book is the narrative of a metamorphosis that we can call a miracle. A miracle that only God can accomplish, and, when it is the true work of God, it will be consistent and without change. Time will show us what was the source that provided the resources for such a metamorphosis.

Nivaldo Nassiff
Brazilian Ministry Pastor, First Baptist Church
Orlando, Florida

"We were meant to be aligned with Him and to live with purpose," writes Diogo Esteves in *The Journey of a Kingsman*. Those words are strong medicine to a man whose spirit is hurt, wounded, and hopeless. Yet Christ makes all the difference in the world to a man. Read this real, raw, and authentic account of how one man was led to a personal relationship with Jesus Christ, and you will see how you, too, can find the journey and adventure you've been looking for all your life!

Dr. Pete Alwinson
Pastor Emeritus and Executive Director, Forge Ministries
Casselberry, Florida

God uses every event in our lives to mold and shape us. We can either run from it and continue to act like immature boys, or we can embrace it and learn to become the men and soldiers God has called us to be. This book is going to be a healing tool for the men who allow the Holy Spirit to bring into the light what needs to be addressed and changed in their own lives.

Jeff Young
Owner, Salon No 3
Euless, Texas

Diogo always impressed me as being a person who knew what he wanted and was fully committed in achieving anything he set his mind to. We met at Florida Christian University back in 2010 or so, where we took some classes together while I was pursuing my MA in coaching. From the outside, one would not imagine Diogo as a person who would be facing the inner crisis he exposes in his book. It took great courage to share the fears and disappointments he has gone through. Only a person who is on the path to victory is able to bring these to light as he has. He shows the importance of having a spiritual mentor as a key in the recovery process. It is a story that many will be able to relate to, and it provides clear steps on how to overcome inner crisis, depression, personal frustration, and most of all: discovering and fulling one's purpose in life.

Tony Wilkins
Pastor, Church in the Son
Apopka, Florida

We as a community of men have covered up our pain so long, and the mission has been critical for so long now, that we don't even know where to begin. Men need to change and become more alive. We have witnessed this need with the uncovering of men acting out in Hollywood this past year. Mentorship is a huge component; we don't know what true success looks like on our own. Diogo's book, *The Journey of a Kingsman,* will help uncover what has been missing.

Joshua Brockman
Business Development
Orlando, Florida

Diogo is a man who has experienced brokenness, which gives him a huge heart for people who are in the same place. Read this work, which is a reflection of the greatness of God. Grab a copy for yourself and a friend!

Trina Titus Lozano
Pastoral Counselor, Kingdom Global Ministries
Colleyville, Texas

Fantastic job! I admire the awareness Diogo has had in his life and how he has been able to translate his learnings into the book to share his experiences with others. I can relate as well, as I have been working the past few years on my own personal development. Having the right mindset, along with the other quests in this book, will serve as a base of personal and career success for those on their Kingsman journey!

Steve Birk
Loan Officer, Strongwealth Mortgage
Orlando, Florida

Millions of people at this very moment are roaming through life, unable to find answers to their most profound life questions. Most end up losing themselves, especially when they end up believing that success—whether financial, professional or personal—is what they have been looking for this entire time.

What would life be like if you could finally find the answers you have been looking for? This is exactly what will happen as you peruse the pages of *The Journey of a Kingsman*. You will be invited to reflect about your own life and apply the life-changing principles shared throughout this book. Diogo opens his heart in a real and raw way, and in the simplest way possible, shares his story of success and struggle, as he finally finds a way to get in touch with his true self, discovering real prosperity and internal peace.

Regardless of where you are in life or even how bad your current situation is, this book will challenge and inspire you to change the way you have been living your life up until this point.

Angela Perrella
Business Woman and Coach
São Paulo, Brazil

What an amazing journey! There is nothing more inspiring than the testimony of someone who has won the fight against himself. Reading this book is like looking at yourself in the mirror, as it is literally impossible not to relate to many of the situations Diogo has gone through. I have no doubt that this story will light up the dark path that many people have been walking on, helping them change their lives around and be able to one day finally achieve their highest goal in life: fulfill their God-given destiny and live a life of freedom and purpose.

Glauber Rangel
Pastor, International Revival Presbyterian Church
Marlborough, Massachusetts

Life is like a journey. We experience patterns of victory and defeat in this adventure, often assuming we are mere objects with no choice in the story. What happens happens. We must just endure it. As men, we work hard to be tough. We try to fight our way through that journey.

I'm a man who knows myself and my tendencies well. I'm a pastor, a counselor, a writer, and a speaker who knows many men well. I see the pain those tendencies and patterns bring.

But I also know about another option. Men are not required to live that way. We can be proactive, pursuing positive outcomes through the choices we make.

In his book and his workshops, Diogo Esteves invites us into what he calls *The Journey of a Kingsman*. His honest narratives, challenging questions, and motivational suggestions provide an exciting look at this life adventure. He offers a view we should see life through. He reveals his own wounds while daring us to not give up.

Diogo Esteves provides practical ways that marriages, careers, spiritual growth, finances, and honesty can guide men from defeat to victory. Men can make the right decisions. Men do not need to live as victims. Men can view themselves as God created them. Men do not need to give up.

The Journey of a Kingsman is for men—young men, old men, all men. Whatever your past decisions and whatever your future dreams, open the pages. Learn from Diogo's stories and his confessions. Receive his wisdom. Embrace his guidance. Join the adventure. Become a Kingsman.

Chris Maxwell
Author, Speaker, and Spiritual Director
Atlanta, Georgia

Principles have the power to elevate one's purpose in life. This book is filled with principles.

Success is not what we do or what we have, but who we are. Who we become is a process. Always learning, always reaching, always growing. These are the real aspects of Diogo's life. Join him on his journey, and write your own story as you experience God's grace in his.

This book is not your finishing line; it is your launching pad to embrace your greatness.

Devi Titus
Author/Speaker; Vice President, Kingdom Global Ministries
Colleyville, Texas

Although I've known Diogo for only a short time, I've seen his drive and combined passion for people create opportunities for many to run in their lanes. In addition, he is passionate about his relationship with the Creator, and it shows in his commitment to those who surround him. After having overcome many adversities, Diogo has demonstrated a grit and determination like few I've known. I'm thankful for him, and I believe this resource will bless you in ways you couldn't have imagined.

Marcus Kenny
Consultant and Creative Director, MK Consulting
Dallas, Texas

I have known Diogo for a few years now and have seen the changes in his life that not only show in him but reflect in his family as well. I encourage anyone who is stuck and looking for a fresh viewpoint and honest approach in moving forward to read *The Journey of a Kingsman*.

John W. Gusti
Program Manager, Trigg GC
Southlake, Texas

Success and failure are defined by each individual and are not final until we declare it so.

Experiencing failure is part of life—once you have experienced it, you need to explore what you have learned, how you have grown, and the lessons you have taken into your life.

In *The Journey of a Kingsman*, Diogo Esteves does a great job of allowing the reader to see how a man in his own journey takes inventory and realizes that it's not a matter of starting over. It's a matter of the new and improved individual getting another chance.

Failure isn't final; it's fertilizer for success, and Diogo's book is a great reminder of this truth.

David Hill
Founder, IronMen of God
Orlando, Florida

Diogo is my oldest brother. Ever since I can remember, he has always been an entrepreneur and a visionary, always shooting for the stars. His character and personality have been shaped over the years, not only by his victories but especially by his failures. We all sometimes need to fail in order to succeed, and this book shows exactly that. The challenges went on for years, before he could finally understand the path he should follow. This book is essential to those who wish to learn from someone else's mistakes and save themselves a lot of time throughout their journey. Truly inspiring. Great job!

Diego Esteves
Manager, Quintal da Disney
Orlando, Florida

I believe every man has a divine call—a role in life he was meant to play. When we live according to that divine call, life becomes rich. Unfortunately, far too many of us get caught up in other things. We get distracted, disillusioned, and sometimes derailed by life. This book is a reminder that we don't have to stay that way. Diogo's story is one of hope and encouragement for men who want to have the best life possible—the life they were born to live!

David Welday
President, HigherLife Publishing
Oviedo, Florida

I've known Diogo and Daniela for nine years now, and I am very excited for their continuous focus to not only get better in their own lives, but to care enough to give guidance to others as well. Throughout life, you are blessed with the opportunity to learn from people who care enough to share their experiences and to help guide you. Listen—it just might make sense! Success leaves a trail. Diogo wants to help you find it!

Robert McCready, Jr.
Senior Vice President, Primerica
Orlando, Florida

I'm positive you will be tremendously blessed and encouraged by reading *The Journey of a Kingsman* by Diogo Esteves. This resource can be life changing to the one who has an open heart to receive from it. Diogo is a dear friend and wonderful man of God whom I respect greatly.

Billy Dalton
Founder, All Things Grace
Tulsa, Oklahoma

Diogo invites you on his meaningful journey and his powerful transformation. His heart smiles at what God has done in his life as he bravely shares it so you can feel the same joy.

"Forgiveness comes through understanding." Diogo has grasped this fully as his life unfolds according to God's plan.

Dr. Don Wood
Founder, Inspired Performance Institute
Orlando, Florida

The Journey of a Kingsman provides much rich and transparent insight into the moments of process and change. My friend and brother, Diogo, imparts a stronger and deeper understanding of purpose…elevating us into higher dimensions in every facet of life. I strongly believe there will be inevitable transformation, joy, and productivity in your living so you can experience your fullest potential in God!

Fernando Alvarez
Founder, Rendered Heart International
Houston, Texas

Endorsing a book always challenges me and fills my heart with joy. My academic years have led me to value authors who are not focused on vanity or superb knowledge but rather those who demonstrate human vulnerability—"The Reality Show," or as I like to call it, "Reality Check"—which is something you will see quite a bit in the book you now hold in your hands.

When Diogo wrote this book, openly sharing his heart, exposing his deepest feelings, and showing how much of an impact discovering God's purpose for him would ultimately have in his life, he was completely aware of the amount of criticism he could potentially receive. But still, he was driven by the need to impact, through his life experiences, the lives of other people, who just like him, still question their life's purpose.

His ultimate goal with this book is not to give you an easy-steps-to-success story, but to be an actual guide and help you make a conscious decision to change for the better. He covers all areas of life that will, at one point or another, need to be developed in order to have the life you were meant to have. I firmly believe that reading this book will allow you to become completely aware of your actual state of mind, empowering you to rethink your future. The way you think about everything in life will completely change.

I deeply admire people who, after having gone through a desert, come out the other side stronger than ever, and this book will surely serve as a compass to those who wish to increase their level of resilience.

Diogo, a creative young entrepreneur and responsible husband and father, exposes in each page of this book his deepest feelings, allowing us to see how he was able to overcome his biggest challenges in life.

The challenge with a book like this is believing that it could trigger something within you that will eventually generate a massive impact, and with that, cause an extraordinary, lifelong, lasting transformation.

Prof. Anthony Portigliatti, PhD
Florida Christian University
President, Board of Directors
Orlando, Florida

I am eternally grateful for what God has done in Diogo's life. Although he has always been a wonderful son, for a period of his life he found himself lost and away from the right path, which brought undesirable things into his life. God only knows how hard he has been working these past few years to become the person he was created to be. As his mother, I couldn't be prouder of what I have seen happen in his life.

We all need to go through life with the understanding that although we might fall, God is right there to pick us back up. We also need to be aware and understand that the only way the first stone can be cast is if we have never made any mistakes ourselves. As his intercessor, I have been praying for him for many years so he could finally find the freedom he was intended to have. Today I am thankful to say: God's mercy has finally reached him. I will keep praying for him, asking God to constantly direct his every step so that He can continue to use Diogo's life for a greater purpose. I thank Him every day for finally bringing my son home. My wish is that this book will reach others who, like him, need this same encounter—I know I do!

God is about to show him and his family something they have never seen before. My wish is that they continue to develop a close relationship with God, listening to His voice and following every direction He gives them.

Rose Esteves
The Author's Mother
Orlando, Florida

We know the author. We know his life, his challenges, struggles, and battles, and above all, how he was able to overcome it all and still come out the other side, victorious. Diogo is our firstborn son, and from an early age, he has always amazed us. He is the type of son any mother and father would love to have. Always sharp, focused, dynamic, smart, handsome (he inherited his good looks from his mom), and aware. I know every parent says that about his or her child, but the truth is, we couldn't be prouder of him.

When he was only twelve years old, Diogo already knew what he wanted in life. He moved to the United States by himself when he was only seventeen years old, and in his first year in this country, surprised us all with the results he was able to achieve. He came back to Brazil to marry his high-school sweetheart so he could then go back to his newfound home. Nothing was easy for him. He wasn't born with a silver spoon in his mouth but always put in the extra effort so he could finally achieve the things he had longed for all his life.

He gave my wife and me our first two American grandsons: Matthew, who is a true miracle and a gift from God, and Lucca, who is simply awesome. They are truly our pride and joy.

Diogo has been through some major battles in his life. The worst of them? A tremendous battle of the mind. It might not seem like much, if you haven't been through anything like this, but trust me, it is the toughest challenge of all. How do I know? I have been there as well.

As the saying goes, with God's grace, even though life gave Diogo lemons, he was able to make a delicious lemonade out of them. He truly is more than a conqueror.

The trials and tribulations he experienced throughout his life, which are shared in *The Journey of a Kingsman,* are at the same time raw and real. They will certainly help and bless anyone who gets a chance to experience this journey—especially those who are currently going through a similar situation. He was able to truly take off the mask and pour his heart and soul into the pages of this book. This is incredible because for the most part, most of us put on masks so others can see how good we are, when in fact Jesus is the only truly good one. After all, He frees and delivers us from evil.

"So if the Son sets you free, you are truly free" (John 8:36).

Humberto Esteves
Real Estate Broker, Seven Realty
Orlando, Florida

THE JOURNEY OF A
KINGSMAN

AND THE 12 QUESTS TO BECOME
THE ONE YOU WERE CREATED TO BE

DIOGO ESTEVES

The Journey of a Kingsman
by Diogo Esteves

Copyright © 2018 The Kingsman Academy
All rights reserved

Published by HigherLife Development Services, Inc.
PO Box 623307
Oviedo, Florida 32762
(407) 563-4806
www.ahigherlife.com

ISBN 978-0-9998197-4-6

Scripture quotations are taken from the Holy Bible, New Living Translation, copyright © 1996, 2004, 2015 by Tyndale House Foundation. Used by permission of Tyndale House Publishers, Inc., Carol Stream, Illinois 60188. All rights reserved.

First Edition
13 14 15 16 17 —12 11 10 9 8 7 6 5
Printed in the United States of America

This journey has been the wildest one I have ever had the opportunity to go on during my entire life. My wife and I have not only been to hell and back; we were also tossed into the fire multiple times to be purified before we could set out to do what God has called us to do. It has been the most difficult process we have ever had to endure. But by His grace, we were able to come out on the other side, victorious.

I am so thankful for the opportunity I've had through this process to connect with so many wonderful people who have contributed to our lives in small or big ways and, more importantly, who have been a source of inspiration and guidance along this journey. We are fully aware of how blessed we are and the privilege we have had to be able to experience this level of care. Like the Father He is, God takes care of His children. He allows us to learn the lessons, yes; but at the same time, He protects us and doesn't allow any harm to come to us. And even though the process may be long and painful, the rewards that come with it are absolutely incredible. This book is an attempt to put into words how appreciative we are for everything He has done for us because if we had planned it all, it would not have worked out as well.

I first want to thank my wife, Daniela, for sticking with me through this whole process and giving me the strength to keep moving forward. Had it not been for her, none of this would have been possible. Had it not been for her, I wouldn't even be here today, literally. The saying is true after all: Behind every great man is a phenomenal woman. She is my rock. She is my everything.

I am also privileged to be the father of the two most amazing kids on Earth, Matthew and Lucca. Everything we do is with them in mind. Every experience I put myself through and every lesson I learn leads me to ask myself how I can pass it along to them in a simple and effective way that will allow them to not only survive this long journey called life but to thrive and achieve anything they set out to accomplish.

To my parents, Humberto and Rose, my eternal gratitude for always doing the best they could for us and providing us with a life that any kid would love to have, not only guiding but also caring for us every step of the way. I thank them for their prayers and support, as I know they played a major role in my life. To my brother and sister, Diego and Desiree, for being there for me when I needed them the most and for holding down the fortress when I was nearly losing my mind and didn't know what to do.

To our mentors and spiritual parents, Larry and Devi, our deepest gratitude for opening the doors to their home at a time that was so crucial. I honestly don't know what we would have done without their guidance, wisdom, and support. God knows we are eternally grateful for everything they have done for us. To their daughter, Trina, who was a key piece in the restoration process of our marriage during a time of desperate need, when we didn't know what to do. We are grateful for her words of wisdom and practical steps toward healing.

To my new friend, Chris, for guiding me every step of the way and helping me craft this beautiful message so I could finally have a chance to share with others what God has done in my life. To David and the entire HigherLife team for the amazing support and for believing that I do have something impactful to share with the world. And to everyone else who was a part of this incredible journey, my deepest appreciation. We love you all dearly and hope to one day be able to contribute to your lives as much as you have contributed to ours.

TABLE OF CONTENTS

When I met Diogo, I met an incredible young man. He is sharp, articulate, handsome, brilliant, driven, and creative. While still in his twenties, he had already done better financially than most people do throughout their lifetimes. By all outward appearances, he was successful. But soon, I learned that he was very broken and falling apart. His success was becoming failure in his marriage, career, fatherhood, and spiritual life—the things that really mattered.

The Journey of a Kingsman is his story, poignantly written, and strikingly like the lives of most of us. The outer shell of his manhood shouts success while the inner reality is drowned in sadness, disappointment, discouragement, emptiness, and ultimate disaster.

In the Epilogue, Diogo shares, "Along this journey, I have shared with you my stories, my dreams, and my lessons. I've revealed to you my purpose and my destiny. Why? Why would I share the most painful parts of my life with you? Why would I expose my weaknesses like that?"

I can answer the "Why?" of Diogo's question: without vulnerability and full exposure of his pretentious past, he could never have experienced the freedom found in his new life. Neither can we. Diogo opens the door to transformation and allows us to walk through with him.

Diogo's journey is part testimonial and part instruction. He identifies lessons he has learned that will benefit every person. When Diogo opens his heart with transparency, uncommon to most people, he allows us to walk with him through the process that God uses to turn every one of us from ordinary to extraordinary—from an average human being to a Kingsman.

Nothing is more instructive than someone's life story. That's why the Book of Revelation says, "And they have conquered him (the devil) by the blood of the Lamb and by the word of their testimony, for they loved not their lives even unto death" (Rev. 12:11, ESV).

Theology can be argued, but it is difficult to disagree with a life that has gone through the fire without the smell of smoke—without bitterness or blame.

It seems impossible for anyone to read this book without being deeply impacted or even transformed. I believe God has a master plan for your life, and that plan will be made much clearer as you peruse the pages of *The Journey of a Kingsman*. You will relate not only to the pain but also to the purpose—God's ultimate plan for your life.

Read this book with a highlighter. Take note of the principles that apply to you. Embrace change. Royalty awaits you.

Larry Titus
President
Kingdom Global Ministries

NOW AND THEN

After all the mental torture I have been through for eight long years, the fact that I am alive today is a tremendous miracle. That alone gives me the drive and the motivation to share my journey with you.

Life is, without a doubt, a true gift from our Creator. But at the same time, unless we can actually live life the way it was meant to be lived and not simply exist, it is nothing but a waste of time and resources. God's purpose in my life is an irresistible call to bring other people like you along the way.

I am not a travel agent sending you to a destination I've never been to before. I want to be your guide—someone who has already been there and is now taking others with him. Because of where my life adventures have taken me, I want you to know how thankful I am for the opportunity you have given me to be your guide on this journey. To show you my appreciation, I am willing to be completely transparent and vulnerable about my own struggles. I want you to know what I've had to face and endure throughout the years. I want you to know what I've had to pursue and overcome so I could be here today.

Unlike some authors, who try to provide you with content that will completely sell you on their points of view and *tell* you *what* to think, leaving you completely clueless and still lost by the time you finish it, my goal with this book is completely different. I want to *show* you *how* to think. I wrote this book to empower you to live life with your eyes and ears wide open.

This gift called life, which every one of us has been given, can be simple or complicated. Although most of the people around us will say that our time here on Earth is full of choices, as I will show you throughout this book, this could not be further from the truth— at least not in the sense that you have been taught all your life.

Having this understanding will completely liberate you. But for that to happen, you will need to understand that the process of reaching your full potential will not be the easiest journey you have ever gone through. I went through it, and it was painful—but it had to happen for me to become aligned with God's purpose for my life.

Is it worth the effort? Absolutely. But it's definitely not easy. I want you to know that before we start on this journey so you understand exactly what's ahead of you. It all starts with changing the way you think and your perspective—how you view most things in life.

This is more than just an inspirational book. I want this book to guide you toward freedom. But please, don't just read it. Don't just look for a quick fix. Don't pursue an easy-steps-to-success story. As you read these pages, I want you to learn how to make a conscious decision to change.

Each quest in *The Journey of a Kingsman* will guide you on a wild adventure of true surrender and ultimate freedom. If you engage in this encounter, your life will drastically change. Your spirit, soul, and

YOU ARE ABOUT TO GRASP A WHOLE NEW REASON FOR LIVING

body will never be the same. The reason you wake up each morning will be different than it was before. The way you think about money will be different. Your relationships and conversations will all change. Why? Because you are about to grasp a whole new reason for living.

To reach that potential, however, I want you to begin thinking correctly while reading this book. Let these thoughts fill your mind to the point that they consume your very being.

Throughout this book, I talk about all the areas in our lives that I believe need to be developed and ultimately mastered if we ever want to become who we were created to be. There is no way around it. Things are not supposed to remain as they've always been. What this book reveals for each quest will help you transform in a way you never thought possible. Now, it is important for you to understand that I don't expect you to agree with everything I am about to share. We all have different personalities, temperaments, gifts, and talents. We all see the world from different perspectives and have different opinions about different subjects at any given time. I am well aware of that. All I ask is that you have an open mind. Allow me to share with you what I have gone through and learned, from my lens and my perspective. These are personal experiences, so take what makes sense for you and apply it to your own life. Remember: I want to *show* you *how* to think, not *tell* you *what* to think.

This process of experiencing a life adventure keeps us on course. We each have a purpose. Life brings meaning. It's not a quick high and then a sudden low. It's about growth, development, and change—all coming from our willingness to surrender and then stay the course for this great adventure.

Too many people spend their lives rushing after the wrong things. *If I could only have that car, I would be happy. If I could only have that house, I would be happy.* We go from a little house to a big house. We go from a good job to a great job. We go from a little bank account to a big bank account. But then what do you think happens when you finally get there? Do you honestly believe you will find what you are looking for? Do you think that's where happiness lives?

When you finally get to what you believe is the top of the mountain, you will finally realize that the great job, the new car, and the big house have been nothing but distractions along the way that have led you to climb the wrong mountain. Most of us have an internal drive to pursue our dreams, which usually come in the form of material things. But we never realize that fulfilling those so-called dreams will never lead us to the true sense of purpose we are looking for. How do I know that? Because I have been there.

The things we so often blindly pursue don't ultimately matter. They are nothing but a bunch of superficial things that will never fulfill our spirits, only our external lives—and temporarily at that. They are nothing but a quick fix—a quick shot of adrenaline that will get us to the next goal. When we finally find our true identity, our true purpose, then all the other things will come into play at the right time. They will be nothing but good fruit. Then, and only then, they will no longer have control over us. Ever.

My goal with this book is to keep you from climbing the wrong mountain. The last thing I want is to see you aggressively pursuing a destiny that God has not designed for you. That is an extremely dangerous journey to embark on. If you end up on that path, you will be exhausted and afraid. Your belief in yourself and even in your Creator will start to dwindle, and you will find yourself completely lost.

So I plead with you—stop climbing the wrong mountain. Stop pursuing a destiny of the enemy's (Satan's) making. Find your purpose. Step into your destiny. Fulfill your calling. Yes, financial resources will come to bless your life, but they will not change you if you stay true to your identity and destiny. God is waiting to bless you, but you must be ready so the blessing does not become a curse in your life.

Most people (if not everyone) would look at a quick cash infusion into their lives—winning the lottery, for example—as a "blessing." But if you do a little research, you will discover that most lottery winners declare bankruptcy just a few short years after coming into a large sum of money and are left in a worse financial situation than they were in before. So, was that lottery win really a blessing? To me, it was a curse because they will now live the rest of their lives with a huge regret, always blaming themselves for squandering the money, when all they really needed was the right preparation to use the money wisely.

That is just one example. There are many situations in life that appear to be blessings at first but turn out to be curses that disrupt God's plan for our lives and cause us misery. Getting into a relationship that seems wonderful at first, landing what appears to be a great new job, or starting a partnership with a business partner in what looks to be a lucrative new start-up are all examples. When we face big life decisions, we need God's wisdom and guidance more than ever.

And Elisha said, "Borrow as many empty jars as you can from your friends and neighbors. Then go into your house with your sons and shut the door behind you. Pour olive oil from your flask into the jars, setting each one aside when it is filled." So she did as she was told. Her sons kept bringing jars to her, and she filled one after another. Soon every container was full to the brim! "Bring me another jar," she said to one of her sons. "There aren't any more!" he told her. And then the olive oil stopped flowing. When she told the man of God what had happened, he said to her, "Now sell the olive oil and pay your debts, and you and your sons can live on what is left over" (2 Kings 4:3-7).

A true Kingsman realizes that he was created by someone superior to himself—he has a clear definition of his Creator. He knows he was created for a specific purpose that he is to fulfill during the time that has been given to him on this Earth. That is what makes you a Kingsman: a clear idea of *who your Creator is, who He says you are,* and *why He created you.* Once you realize that, you will begin a process to reach your full potential. This process is fulfilled by mastering the twelve quests.

An old saying tells us that, to find the pot of gold, we must follow the rainbow until the end. Like most people, I could say I have all the answers you need and simply hand you a specific map that would allow you to eventually reach your ultimate destination. I would, however, be creating a false sense of hope and by the time you were done reading this book, you wouldn't feel any different. It is important to keep in mind what I have shared with you in the beginning: I am not here to *tell* you *what* to think but rather to *show* you *how* to think.

I wrote *The Journey of a Kingsman* to help you find, understand, and navigate the map that was created specifically for you. It is about showing you ways to not only find it but also to follow it. What is your map showing you? I want to be your guide and help you understand what it is showing you so you can be clear about what the next step is. If you are like me, you want to take the time to find, understand, and follow your map. You will find the pot of gold at the end of the rainbow. That is what so many

BEING A KINGSMAN IS LIKE HEAVEN ON EARTH TO ME

people are searching for. We all want to know who we are and why we are here. Why else would we wake up each morning? Without the map, life would be meaningless and simply not worth living.

Being a Kingsman is like heaven on Earth to me. It is why we were created to begin with. I believe it is the only way to fulfill our true purpose in life. That is the journey I am about to take you on. It is all about understanding who your Creator is, who you truly are, and what your mission on Earth really is.

QUEST ONE
PURPOSE

CHAPTER 01

From Submission to Release

How did you feel as you woke up this morning?

The alarm clock roused you from a night of sleep. Or maybe you were lying in bed awake, and hearing the alarm clock caused you to dread getting up to face a new day. Maybe you have learned the routine well—you grab a few more minutes of sleep and then finally force yourself to scramble out of bed to endure another daily routine. You grab some food. You take a quick shower and get dressed. You get in the car and enter your ordinary world. Another day, nothing new, no real purpose, just enduring and existing.

Don't you sometimes ask yourself, "Isn't there more to life than this?" I know that feeling.

Maybe you are one of those ambitious people who is eager to wake up each day on a mission to pursue your goals—money, fame, security, or pleasure. But don't you ever get exhausted from all of this?

WHY ARE YOU HERE ON THIS PLANET?

Assess How Happy You Are Right Now

What is life really about? Why are we here? Why are *you* here on this planet? How do *you* feel when you wake each day?

If you told me what you do for a living, would I hear energy in your voice? Or dread? If you talked to me about your family, would I hear contentment? Or guilt? If you described to me your relationship with God, would your tone indicate joyful hope? Or religious duties?

These questions reveal our personal realities. Our answers expose our present life conditions. Even if we love our spouse and children, our jobs, the people we work with, our gifts, and our God, pleasure is temporary. We need more. We need much more than the routine, more than the ritual. You were made for more!

You and I need a purpose to drive us, to inspire us, to thrill us, to dare us, to challenge us. We need a purpose of value. We need a purpose that affects everything we do every day of our lives. We need a reason to wake up, to drive to the office, to engage in conversations, to finish business deals, to invest our time. We desperately want to not just *be*. We need a quest for what we can *become*.

Why did you wake up this morning? What is your true motive for doing what you do each day? What is your purpose? In Ecclesiastes, we read that life is all meaningless. I believe that is true, unless we can find and fulfill our God-given purpose in life. If we live without a purpose, we are going to be miserable until we can finally grasp it. Or, if not miserable, at least numb. That is our lot in life—until we finally realize that we were all uniquely created and given amazing gifts and talents to be able to fulfill our specific and special purposes in life.

Imagine Being Driven By a Sense of Purpose

Imagine for a moment what life would be like if you truly believed God has a plan for you—and you knew exactly what it was. Think about waking up each morning, aware of the true reason you are here. You hear the alarm clock but are already awake after a good night of sleep. Something is driving you to open your eyes, eat a healthy breakfast, sing a joyful song, go through an amazing workout, get in the shower, pray with your family, and finally drive to work, with a deep smile in your heart rather than a fake smile forced by your method of faking joy.

You aren't shoved by guilt; you're stimulated by healthy ambition. You realize God has created you with a purpose. You accept the truth that you were crafted and called for such a time as this—this morning, this day, this very moment.

Thinking this way changed my thoughts and my view of life. Thinking this way changed me. It can change you, too. Knowing and living in your purpose can align your life. You can follow a specific plan tailored just for you. How awesome would it be to wake up each morning knowing there is a specific purpose in each area of your life? Think of viewing life as more than just putting forth an effort to better budget your money, eat better, and exercise more often. Think of viewing life from a better lens—one that inspires you, one that gives a true reason for all you are doing.

Too many times, we miss this type of motivation, don't we? We keep seeking external factors to serve as our adrenaline. We need a thrill here and a high there to motivate us. We watch TV for six hours a day. We overeat. We are unhappy at home, at work, and in church. We live with no goals. But imagine waking up every day, eager to step into another day of your destiny. It changes everything—living with a calling rather than deriving temporary happiness from external things. This realignment reveals our true destiny. We can live with a constant, abiding sense of wellness and joy that is just there, no matter what happens around us. Unshakable. Unmovable.

Instead of getting thrills from buying a new car or buying a new house, what I hope for you is a glimpse of what is possible. A peek behind the curtain to see just how amazing your life can be. You, living a life that truly matters. Not temporary thrills but permanent purpose. True destiny. We realize that our names matter, our lives matter, and our stories matter. But the other stuff always wears off. A new high. A new event. A new thrill. A new job. External factors do not change us from the inside.

But when your spirit grasps true life purpose, the world had better watch out. You change, and you change the world around you. You wake up each day with ambitions—healthy, joyful, ambitions to serve, care, and love. You cry when you should cry. You laugh when it is time to laugh. You wake up each day answering the question of why you are here. Your spirit inspires your mind to think correctly and creatively. It guides your soul and body to live appropriately.

Align Your Daily Activities with Your Life's Purpose

Think about it this way. When I go to the chiropractor, I look great on the outside. I'm well-dressed and standing as tall as I can. I even have a smile on my face. But something is off. Something hurts. When I am worn down by old habits, my body gets bogged down. My spine is misaligned, something is out of place, and my body can't quite function

I MUST ADDRESS THE ISSUES CAUSING MY PAIN

like it is meant to. I should not leave it alone and pretend all is well. I must address the issues causing my pain. I must be willing to be realigned.

If my external frame sometimes needs a realignment, then imagine my internal frame. That mystical part of me that drives everything—my heart and mind—sometimes needs alignment, too. Aligning my daily activities around my purpose is the ultimate key to living life how it was supposed to be lived.

It's pretty simple. If I choose to ignore my situation, my life as a whole will only get worse as each day goes by, and I will once again waste valuable time.

If we deny our present life situations, if we deny our true purpose for being here, if we ignore what matters most, we get worse.

Here is another way to think about it. Right now, I am staring at a clock made of pure gold. Its arms are intricately cut out of precious metal, and its face is crafted of pure mother-of-pearl. The frame is ornate and rich. It's the perfect adornment for its resting place on the wall.

But it doesn't display the right time. The ticking mechanism in its heart is missing, and the only way to repair it is to return it to the clockmaker who designed it. The timepiece can't tell time unless this mechanism is inserted by someone who knows the inner workings of this particular clock's gears. The centerpiece can be found only in the shop where the clock was made. The creator of this timepiece must animate it, or else it will never tell time as it was meant to do.

My grandfather, who is no longer with us, owned a farm in Brazil and spent all his life wanting to grow oranges. I remember vividly that he also loved to play the lottery, hoping for a stroke of luck and maybe get his orange grove up and running. Truth is, he never won, but he would invest quite a bit of money from his day job into his orange dream. But after years and years of pouring into that dream, he was never able to produce a single dollar of profit.

Put yourself in his place for a moment. We all do that in different ways. What was he looking for? I can't help but ask myself whether or not he had a true sense of happiness and fulfillment.

Discover Who You Really Are—In Christ

That was me for the longest time. I was also caught up in what I was doing and what I was earning. Nothing more, nothing less.

But that was not *who* or *what* I needed to be—or who I was meant to be. In a single moment, my identity changed. When I fell to my knees and fully surrendered to the One who created me, my spirit came to life. I released what had held me back for so long. I began a process of recovery in which my spirit would now start influencing my soul. Yes, there was a lot of tension between this new spirit and the habits of an old soul. But I released unneeded luggage. I started over. I had finally found a way to start on the journey that would eventually lead me to my ultimate purpose in life. You can, too.

By picking up this book, you have decided to change your story. You must refuse to be controlled any longer by this false identity that has been sold to you all this time. You can pursue the right dreams based on who you really are.

Sometimes I still wake up in the morning feeling that tug to roll back over and stay in bed. We all do, don't we? I drag myself into the day, unsettled, struggling to find excitement for the day's tasks. The difference now is that I know I can reach out and reconnect with my Creator. I know He has the answers I'm looking for. He reminds me of what I already know.

But the Holy Spirit produces this kind of fruit in our lives: love, joy, peace, patience, kindness, goodness, faithfulness, gentleness, and self-control. There is no law against these things! (Gal. 5:22-23).

Then I remember: my spirit is perfect. I am not my body and not my soul. "You *are* a spirit, you *have* a soul, and you *live* in a body," He says to me. "You have connected with Christ now, which means you are now connected with me, your Creator. Your spirit was dead, and that death ran your life. Your body felt heavy like a corpse you had to drag around. And your soul was corroded by the death in your spirit."

I remember what He is telling me. God speaks directly to my thoughts before I can articulate them. "You may not always feel the joy in your soul that defines you, but it still defines you nevertheless. You have the excitement in your spirit. But be patient, as my Word says you are.

Remember that your soul and body must now catch up to your spirit. You are alive. You have love, joy, peace, patience, kindness, goodness, faithfulness, gentleness, and self-control. This is your true nature."

When you start to feel down, you must remind yourself, "That's not who I am. The Bible says that I am patient, good, and faithful." You must keep thinking about purpose, purpose, purpose. You must choose to retrain your mind to think of yourself as this: a new person who is discovering a true purpose.

"Be patient, son," He says. "I am a God of order, organization, and steps. You are on a journey, and your chariot cannot go in front of the horses, or you will not arrive at your destination."

Recognize That Recovery Is a Journey

My recovery is a journey, I realize. I am on a path. I am facing the right direction now. I am connected to the source of all purpose; I know my Creator. There is light where there was darkness. There is life where I was dying before. There is desire where there was hopelessness. There is life in my eyes. My body is already catching on. He is right. I will follow.

I sit up and get started with my day. As I do, the mundane tasks of getting ready and leaving the house begin to feel like steps toward something bigger. I get in the car and turn on the radio to hear my life set to music. The words resonate, and I am reminded of what He tells me I am. The song "My Recovery" by Unspoken narrates to me my own surrender—what happened when I fell to my knees in my darkest moment. The steps start to make sense to me now. I am sitting still, not simply because I am in a moving vehicle on the way to perform a task, but still *inside*. My soul is beginning to feel at rest; my spirit is finally flooding the darkness with light. I am still, and I can feel my heart beating. I feel full.

Listen to the song "My Recovery" today. Listen to it right now. Let God be the one who recovers you. This will be the beginning of your new adventure from submission to release. This will inspire you in the pursuit of fulfilling your true purpose and reaching your destiny.

I know. There are times when this journey feels like a trek through the desert. The heat and dryness are overwhelming to my senses, but I finally feel like I am moving toward an oasis, a place where that desolation is out of place. This journey could take forty years or twelve days. And I have a strong sense that if I simply do as God is bidding me, and believe that He is doing the work that needs done, I will get through the desert in a matter of days.

> *The LORD was angry with Israel and made them wander in the wilderness for forty years until the entire generation that sinned in the LORD's sight had died (Num. 32:13).*

But people of God acting as his mouthpieces sweep into my life, reminding me, "You are strong, you are intelligent, you are good." His

THE RUBBLE OF THE DEAD SPIRIT CLEARS AWAY

truth overrides the trauma of your past; He redeems time. The rubble of the dead spirit clears away as the truth builds a proper foundation to rebuild life in Him.

Evaluate Your Motives

Imagine what life would be like every day if you wanted to go to work, wanted to live and not simply exist. If someone offered you a totally different job that paid you a lot more money, but it was something you did not enjoy, would that fulfill your purpose just because it brought more money? Would it therefore give you a "better life"? If someone offered you a large amount of money and you took the job, you would be living a lie.

The truth is, many people are addicted to money and what it can give them. I surely was. Take a moment to evaluate your true motives and the reason behind every decision you have ever made. What would you want people to say about you long after you are gone? Would they even say anything at all? What kind of legacy would you like to leave behind?

Take that moment now. Glance in the mirror. How do you view yourself? How does God view you?

He has created you. He has called you. My father always said that God will do His 99 percent if you do your 1. He will do His part if you do yours. God has given you desires He wants you to pursue. He is real in your everyday life. Don't over-spiritualize it; see God in the moments. He has a better view from the top of the mountain. He wants you to see life His way.

This book invites you into an adventure of pursuing your destiny. Your entire life is about to change—your finances, your thinking, your marriage, your ministry, your job, your relationships, and your self-talk.

The person you are meant to be is not who you think you are now. It is who God has called and designed you to be. Your spirit needs to be unlocked to affect your soul and your body. Begin to see yourself in a new mirror—who you really are in the spirit, designed by God. This recovery process doesn't need to be so frustrating and last forty years; it could come to pass in twelve days if you only believe and do your part.

We were meant to be aligned with Him and to live with purpose. We were meant to live the life He created us to live, not merely to exist.

Steps on The Journey of a Kingsman

Let's review the steps from this chapter that will lead you to your ultimate goal of becoming a Kingsman:

1. Assess how happy you are right now. What needs to change?

2. Imagine being driven by a sense of purpose. How would your life be different?

3. Align your daily activities with your life's purpose.

4. Discover who you really are—in Christ.

5. Recognize that recovery is a journey.

6. Evaluate your motives. What are you really trying to accomplish?

CHAPTER 02

The Power of Clarity

I wandered through the empty house. My wife was out, and the kids were still at school. This afternoon was the perfect chance to hatch my plan. I'd been researching this for months now, carelessly Googling sly ways to off myself without leaving a trail of evidence or pain for my family.

A Miserable, Suicidal Existence

For days, I had been wrapped up in the cold, cotton sheets in bed, alone in the guest room. Distant from my family. Locked away. Aimless. I can't even remember if I ate or slept. If I slept, it was an involuntary reaction to purposelessness. I felt lost and frustrated. No one had seen me in a couple of days. When I woke up, a looming sense of destruction awoke with me.

My only wish was not to live long enough to go back to bed that night.

An endless cycle of depression had spiraled into two weeks of this and then two weeks of forcing myself out of bed to do something productive. I wasn't even sure what I was doing, let alone whether it was productive or not. I'd fall into bed, weary of life, feeling the effort it took to draw each breath. That uncertainty always landed me back in bed, trying to sleep away my life, unable to get out of bed, screaming when my thoughts overcame me.

My depression robbed my family and me of a normal life for eight years. I told Daniela bits and pieces of what was going through my mind, probably about 10 percent of it. I thought that if I shared with her the full extent of my agony, it would make her go nuts. She knew I had suicidal thoughts, but not how often or how bad they were. I was able to interact with her and my children, but it was on and off. I spent most of my time by myself and even slept in a separate room upstairs.

Occasionally, when I was alone, I would get up and wander around the house, wearing only the shorts I'd been sleeping in, slamming my arms into the walls, punching the door frames, yelling at no one in particular.

Sometimes I would cry. Sometimes I would scream. The fresh air was hot, and the sunlight seemed to burn my flesh.

On this day, the air felt stiff, heavy. It was dense with the heat of Florida and my dreary thoughts. There was a Hyde-like monster within me; I could feel him scratching at the inner walls of my soul, destroying

I WAS BECOMING A BEAST

me from the inside out in his attempts to escape. I was becoming a beast.

I roamed the house aimlessly, talking to myself. Eventually I wandered up the stairs to my bedroom retreat. Punching the banister with every step, I climbed painfully toward the loft. I ended up turning left at the landing, into our luscious entertainment room. The curtains on the windows were all pulled open, and light was streaming into the room in warm blankets. But I didn't mind.

My favorite room in our house is the home theater room. Although I take a lot of courses, attend a lot of seminars, and read a lot of books, my biggest lessons, especially when it comes to our purpose on Earth, come from movies. I simply love watching good movies with strong messages that get you to take action. Imagine…someone spends $100 million and months, if not years, to produce a film that, in less than two hours, will grab your attention and teach you a valuable lesson. It's amazing that a movie can hold someone's attention for that long in the world we live in today, where everyone suffers from the "shiny-object syndrome."

I meandered into the theater room, perhaps because it was the only one that gave me a glimpse of purpose external to myself. I banged my head against the wall, hoping that by punishing myself, I could keep that alien goblin from breaking free. In the reflection of the TV as wide as I am tall, I felt small and hideous.

My head was aching from the impact, and a tingle of numbness raced up my arms. A surge of pain flowed through my veins every time I punched something. I paced the room, a dramatic performance for two rows of theater seats with no one and nothing occupying them except my guilt, my apathy, and my rage. I had become paralyzed by the fear that anything I did—even ending my life—would simply be indexed in a catalog of all my failings, all my destructive behavior that had plagued my wife and children for eight long years.

My Last Hope: Crying Out to God

I trembled, faltered, compelled to vent my desperation to the only God I knew, yet uncertain of that God's existence. My agnosticism of the previous few months culminated in a confused battery of emotion. I couldn't bring myself to perform the final act. My mind was too engaged. The monster wanted to live.

I had rehearsed my failings and my apologies for them, but making amends was an enormous task; my body buckled under the burden of its enormity. Weak from months of immobility, my knees hit the plush carpet, and the rest of my body slumped along behind. I doubled over in excruciating pain and waved my arms at the ceiling. The grief of failure was evolving into rage at my inability to continue living.

"God, if you're *even real*," I screamed at the top of my lungs, desperate, finally admitting I was even questioning His existence, "either give me purpose, or take my life!" I was a wild beast, howling. I looked up. *"I can't do this anymore!"* My voice was foreign to me; it had not sounded so resolute in longer than I could remember. It was as though my voice was the only thing that could save my children. Its volume was unbearable.

Something in me softened. The questions of God's existence were beginning to find answers in my knee-jerk reaction to a near-death experience. Prayer had reopened the channels. Clarity finally came.

No audible response met my outburst. There was simply a feeling that the monster was on his way out. Something else was replacing the gnarly beast that had eaten away my desire to live. I was aware, if only subconsciously, that there was something better. I felt warm, cared for. The conviction I had had since childhood that I was special began to make sense.

"Do whatever You have to do, and I'll just follow, I'll just obey you," I said. I could feel the beast within me shrinking back. Maybe everything my parents had raised me to believe about the invisible, spiritual world was true after all. "But God, I've got to feel like I'm living my purpose. I've gotta feel like I'm useful, like I'm doing something bigger than myself."

In that moment, I was the agent of my own surrender. I was too weak to end my life, and somehow in that weakness, I had managed to calm the monster and voice all my questions to my Maker. The connection, that experience, changed everything. I was special after all. I was uniquely created. There was a job for me to do on this Earth. The Creator provided the light; I just needed to find it.

I Began to Heal Instantly

A detoxification had begun. The little monster, though he had shrunk, was still there, and would have to be extracted by continual, painful procedures. But in this moment, I knew that was a possibility. I knew there could be something bigger than myself that I could exist for. And even as I became aware of the world outside myself, and my soul was free from the deathlike beast that had held it down for so long, I knew that the Creator was *my* Creator. I had clarity for the first time in my life.

You made all the delicate, inner parts of my body and knit me together in my mother's womb. Thank you for making me so wonderfully complex! Your workmanship is marvelous—how well I know it (Ps. 139:13–14).

The light flooding into the windows began to feel warm. I had given my life to Christ, and a new identity was being revealed already.

Now, every time I closed my eyes, the same image overtook my mind's eye. He was trying to tell me something. My eyelids would fall, and a vision would take the place of the room around me: shards of what used to be a clay vase.

Everywhere I turned, the image of that broken vase appeared. I probably needed the insight of someone who was used to God communicating with people. It was clear to me that the uniqueness of my existence was really *care*—true care coming from my Creator that I had never understood before.

I knew you before I formed you in your mother's womb. Before you were born I set you apart and appointed you as my prophet to the nations. (Jere. 1:5).

But this image would come to provide direction and a theme for my life, the purpose I needed to create the drive to fulfill a specific role.

I had been spinning my wheels, asking questions, aimless yet successful by all accounts. I was well-connected, to say the least. Now I was having this intense vision and feeling an inexplicable draw toward Texas.

And yet, O LORD, you are our Father. We are the clay, and you are the potter. We all are formed by your hand (Isa. 64:8).

My response was an almost apathetic surrender. The responsibility to make decisions for myself, knowing there was someone to guide me now, made me tremble. "Take over my emotions, take over my will, take over my mind. Take over everything because I just simply don't care anymore; I just want to do what You want for me," I found myself pleading.

You made me; you created me. Now give me the sense to follow your commands.
(Ps. 119:73).

God Had Already Planned My Next Move

I needed advice. But out of 284 pastors' numbers I could have called, I dialed the one man from Brazil—where I grew up—with whom I was least acquainted. Marciano was his name. God was answering my request, and I was experiencing the freedom of following the guidance of the Holy Spirit.

When I reached him, I gushed the painful account of my encounter with God in which I gave my life over and asked for purpose. I sobbed through the story. This rawness was going to sting for a while. I caught my breath and worked up the words to tell him about the magnetic attraction to Texas.

"I don't know why, I have no idea, but I'm feeling this crazy attraction to Texas. I don't know anyone there; I have no business there. There's nothing in Texas." I tossed the idea to him like a handful of rice I was hoping would stick to something.

And it stuck.

He had a friend from Texas who was going to travel to Brazil for a conference. "Coincidentally or not, in two days, these pastors with an international ministry are having a conference here, and I want to talk to them about you," Marciano said.

He did. His friend, Larry Titus, asked to meet me. He called me back, astounded by the connections developing so uniquely. Things were starting to fall together like they belonged. Maybe I had been created for a purpose and simply needed to connect with the Creator to realize it.

When I got hold of Larry, he said, "Come out here. I want to meet you."

I spent the three days before my trip to Dallas reading Larry's book, *The Teleios Man.* I wanted to be sure I had read all of it before I met him in person. When I did finally meet him, he didn't have a voice. He had just gotten back from a trip to Africa and ended up contracting something that disabled him from speaking. So I went to lunch with his wife, Devi, and her assistant instead. After lunch, I drove to Larry's home to meet him in person. I looked up to him already, a man with such a clear, strong voice as the author of this insightful work. It spoke volumes that everything he said came out in a whisper. He gave me a hug like I had never received before. He welcomed me into his home like the prodigal son.

My Passion for Life Returns

And then in that raspy whisper, Larry prayed over me, and I found a new kind of voice as the Holy Spirit descended on me. In that new baptism of the Spirit, I felt connected in a new way. There was a passion

I FOUND A NEW KIND OF VOICE AS THE HOLY SPIRIT DESCENDED ON ME

now, a fire inside me where there had been a black hole before, life and warmth where I had been dead and cold, light where there had been darkness.

"I'd love to have you guys next to us," Larry whispered. He was going to fill the role of a mentor. I was no longer alone, not simply within myself. I was becoming a member of a community, like an appendage to a body. Larry knew how to perform the duties of a hand in that body, and he could show me how to do the same.

I still find it fascinating how everything happened. In April, I gave my life to Christ. The next month, I started sensing an attraction to Texas. At the end of June, I spoke to my pastor friend in Brazil. In July, I connected with Larry's assistant. I drove from Florida to Houston in August to begin a three-month program—two months in Houston and one month in Dallas—for a ninety-day real estate course. I met Larry for the first time in Dallas.

In September, the whole family flew to Dallas to meet Larry and Devi. I was still in Houston but drove to Dallas for an event Larry was hosting. Then, on the last part of my three-month program in Dallas, Larry asked me to stay with him during that time. That was like an ER experience to me; all my open wounds would now get a chance to heal. Soon after that, I moved the entire family to Texas.

God had all the pieces working together. His timing. His guidance. His connections. There was no way to plan it. If I had tried, it wouldn't have worked out. Voiceless himself, Larry had been a mouthpiece for the voice of God, imparting me with a voice from God that I had never heard before. I had clarity.

What might have been an eternal traverse through a desert quickly turned into a short walk to an oasis.

And the very hairs on your head are all numbered. So don't be afraid; you are more valuable to God than a whole flock of sparrows (Luke 12:7).

Have you been roaming the house of your life aimlessly? Have you been wrestling a monster within you? Have you felt cold, distant, locked away? Now it's your turn. This is your day. To listen, to learn, to gain clarity. It is your time to grasp your purpose. Now is the opportunity to begin your walk to an oasis, to a Dallas, to a Larry, to a life. Do not miss it!

CHAPTER

02

Steps on The Journey
of a Kingsman

Let's review the steps from this chapter that will lead you to your ultimate goal of becoming a Kingsman:

1. Instead of waiting until you are a miserable, suicidal mess, cry out to God now so you can begin healing and living according to His plan for your life now.

2. Instead of roaming the house of your life aimlessly and wrestling monsters, surrender your struggles to God and accept His love, grace, and redemption into your life.

QUEST TWO
SPIRIT

CHAPTER 03

Our Need For Relationships

Why on Earth would you get in the car at 6:00 a.m. on a Monday to go meet with a group of men?

I recently started doing that with a group of Christian friends, realizing the importance of the Kingsman perspective. So many feel alone; so many battle alone; so many are alone. Too many people believe life is meaningless and that they have nothing to offer. This chapter is about those who need true friends, mentorship, biblical reality, and to face their undeveloped senses. It is about grasping the truth of what we are really like in the eyes of our Creator.

I meet the men in this group weekly because every Sunday night, before going to bed, I remember what it was like to wake up the next day and start my week, not having a single drop of excitement or direction on where I was going or what I was doing that would help me get to my next goal. Every Monday, we meet at the Citrus Club in Orlando for about an hour. Anywhere from three to twelve men attend these get-togethers. These are informal meetings. Typically, the man in the group who has a pressing issue just begins talking, telling us what challenges or victories he had the previous week.

Then we all pitch in and offer our suggestions, support, and encouragement. For example, during a recent meeting, one of our members revealed that he was struggling with the fact that his relationship with his father wasn't what it should be like. But hey, everyone is like this right? It's normal, isn't it? Not at all. And that is one of the biggest problems in our society today—the father wound. He wasn't 100 percent clear on why that was, but he knew that something was off. Because he had been brought up like most people all his life, he was taught that men don't cry, don't show emotions or even ask for help. He was taught that he should just toughen up and figure it out on his own, so he struggled immensely with reaching out every time he had something he didn't know how to handle.

After a few days, he was able to not only expose what he was going through but also reconnect with his father, and that brought an amazing sense of accomplishment. He learned that his father did the best he could with what he had. He also learned that everything had happened for a reason and couldn't have happened any other way. He learned that he is who he is today because of things like this. That helped him

> # EVERYTHING HAD HAPPENED FOR A REASON

understand it, expose it, and heal the wound. His father was a great provider but was emotionally absent all his life. He was also not a mentor and didn't teach our friend how to navigate through life.

Was his father like that because he wanted to be? Absolutely not. He learned that his father also didn't have these two things in his life; therefore, was unable to give what he didn't have.

One incredibly valuable benefit of these meetings is that sharing openly, without fear of judgment, enables us all to become more aware of our undeveloped senses and tap into feelings and emotions we didn't realize we had.

Relationships with Others Enhance Our Relationship with God

Our relationships with ourselves, our families, and our mentors enhance our relationship with God. Our spirits must connect with God—and it happens as we completely surrender ourselves and allow Him to develop us through all other relationships. You will read more about mentorships in a later chapter, but we can understand it correctly only if we fully grasp the meaning of undeveloped senses.

Relationships enable us to cry and laugh—together. Not in isolation. Not feeling abandoned. But together. Loved. Accepted. Important. Sharing hardships and successes. Trying to figure out life. Living life like a true family.

Where are you in that story? If you drove today at 6:00 a.m. to meet with a group of people, what would you be looking for? Wouldn't you want community, healing, acceptance? Wouldn't you crave transparency, accountability, prayer?

I meet so many people who want to hear about this. They want to connect. They want to tell their stories. They want to be healed.

Don't we all want to be healed? Don't we all live desperate lives— seeking to see our spirits awakened as we enter The Journey of a Kingsman?

Thinking about your undeveloped senses can help you begin healing.

Healing from "Father Wounds"

I often speak about "father wounds"—those painful wounds we suffer when our fathers fail to give us the love, security, and approval we seek so desperately as children and beyond. Whenever I do, I see people being drawn into the story. They can relate. We are all imperfect people raised by imperfect ancestors. But our Heavenly Father is healing our hurts and restoring us into the family. Rather than being divided because of imperfection, we can grasp the truth about it and be healed. We can find purpose and meaning. We can understand our calling.

What does your relationship with your earthly father look like? How does that affect your relationship with God, your Heavenly Father? Does your experience with your earthly father cause you to doubt God? Most people answer those questions in ways that confirm the importance of this chapter. I long to see their spirits come alive. I want to see them releasing past hurts related to earthly fathers and find total freedom in their Heavenly Father.

I recently asked a group of men, "On a scale of one to five, with five being that your earthly father is a friend and mentor to you and one being a nonexistent relationship, how would you answer?" As you can probably imagine, I didn't hear any high numbers. I noticed deep disappointment.

They all mentioned similar struggles. Trying to support their families but wrestling to know what to do next in life. Craving a life with true meaning, a life in which they can truly make a difference. Are your thoughts similar to what they said? "I'm feeling unhappy where I am in my life." "My job doesn't seem to match my gifts and talents." "I'm just going through the motions." "I'm too tired from work to invest energy in my family." "I feel like I have no value in life." "I don't think I'm making much of a difference."

Maybe you can relate to a few of their confessions. I want to challenge you as I challenged them.

Throughout *The Journey of a Kingsman*, I will be telling you more about my personal story. But please notice the importance of what I am revealing here. This can change your life. My story will help you write your story and find your true calling. It will dare you to pursue that destiny as you realize that your spirit craves to connect with God's Spirit.

Though it wasn't easy, it wasn't as difficult as I made it to be. I had this belief that if something was going to get done, it was totally up to me. What I didn't realize was that I had been running on fumes my entire life. I was spreading myself too thin, like I was always trying to prove something to someone, although I didn't know to *whom* or *what* exactly. I asked my dad why he believed I had this feeling. I thought maybe he had pushed me hard when I was a kid because I had a constant sense of needing to prove myself. But he said he never did.

It felt as if I needed to do something more, that no matter what I did, it was never enough. I felt like I had to do so much more if I were to ever feel loved—by my earthly father, my Heavenly Father, and anyone else around me.

It was a constant feeling of needing to prove something to someone so I could be accepted and finally fit in. I couldn't see then what I can now—that there's nothing so good or so bad that I can do that will make

BY HIS STRIPES, I *WAS* ALREADY HEALED

my Heavenly Father love me more or love me less. He has already given me everything I need to live an amazing life in this world. He already paid the price, so I don't have to. By His stripes, I *was* already healed.

> *But he was pierced for our rebellion, crushed for our sins. He was beaten so we could be whole. He was whipped so we could be healed (Isa. 53:5).*

Our Circumstances Do Not Define Us

You and I cannot allow our feelings or circumstances to dictate who we are. We must have our spirits connect with our purpose and live with that in mind—all day, every day. No matter what happens around us, we are to be unshakable.

How does this apply to you? Let your spirit awaken. Change your perspective, and you'll change the world. Whatever your age. Whatever your story. Listen to your calling. Pursue your destiny.

We all need a Savior. Refuse to allow anything else to invade that truth. I don't believe life needs to be complicated; I just believe that because of our lack of knowledge, we end up making it way more complicated than it really is. Think about it. Jesus, fully God yet fully human, came to Earth to give His life for sins we had already committed. He established a relationship with us. Why do we have such a hard time with the fact that someone did something good for us? As believers, we need to understand that Jesus came into the world and died for our sins—period. I believe that if we want to fully understand that, we will first need to fully accept it as truth and allow other people to pour grace into our lives as well.

Being with those men helps me understand how much we need this. People are hurting so much; they feel as if they have no voice in this world and that no matter what they say or do, nothing will change. They were not fulfilling their calling. What did they need to do? Realize that there is a plan for them.

Who is helping you understand your spirit's desire for God? Who is asking you the difficult questions that will empower you in new ways?

Let this sink deep in your heart. Instead of placing blame, see life differently. Choose to believe that your earthly father did the best he could. Maybe he did not know how to mentor you properly. Maybe he did not know how to guide you along the way because he was never guided himself. Forgiveness is a choice, a decision. It can set you free, even though it isn't pleasant to face. I once heard T. D. Jakes, the bishop of The Potter's House, a nondenominational American megachurch in Dallas, talk about seeds growing only when crap is thrown at them. It becomes fertilizer. Yes, it smells. Yes, it is ugly. But it is the one thing that allows that seed to grow into something extraordinary.

Pain Comes with Growth

God recently used a very painful season in my life to give me a full detox—to get all the crap, the smells, and death out of my life. I will share this story with you in detail in later chapters.

> # GOD RECENTLY USED A VERY PAINFUL SEASON IN MY LIFE TO GIVE ME A FULL DETOX

Painful stories from the past can inspire our spirits toward a harvest. Death turns into life. We should never be satisfied unless we can fully feel our spirits rejoice.

I didn't realize all this until that instant I got down on my knees and asked God to take my life. But the reason nothing made sense was because, up until that point, I had been going through life deaf, dumb, and blind. The perspective I had of what life should be like was based on the twisted perspective I had of someone who had eyes but couldn't see, had ears but couldn't hear, had a mouth but couldn't speak. It wasn't until that moment that my eyes, my ears, and my mouth were opened, and I finally started becoming aware of what was going on. But it was just the beginning.

I looked at an image of three skeletons. One was deaf. One was dumb. One was blind. That reminded me again of how most people go through life.

Anyone with ears to hear should listen and understand! (Matt. 11:15)

Having clarity about this is crucial. As long as you are deaf, dumb, and blind, you will always go through life not knowing what is going on.

You'll always allow your circumstances to dictate how you live, what you do, and who you become.

Understanding that our spirits are already fully grown, mature, and perfect is crucial. We are not like babies, who need to be nurtured until they are fully mature. Living within us, after all, is the same spirit that raised Jesus from the dead. We have as our guide the Holy Spirit, who was sent to Earth to escort us every step of the way.

There's really no point trying to figure it all out on our own. It's just a matter of connecting to the Source and enjoying the ride. And, although it is full of ups and downs and a true learning process, it's an amazing experience. Your soul and body will eventually have to surrender to the Spirit.

We Do Not Need to Earn God's Love

When the subject of pornography comes up, we often say, "You shouldn't do that." We rarely talk about the scientific side. It is an addiction, after all. The brain's chemistry is changed through pornography. It develops a false sense of pleasure. It changes your perspective of women. It twists everything.

When we look at the spiritual side, the same thing applies. Just as we can get hooked on pornography—a false sense of pleasure, a false idea of expectations and desires—we can get hooked on dangerous teachings on the spiritual side as well.

One of the most dangerous teachings out there is that we must force ourselves to do things to earn God's love, that God will not love us unless we (fill in the blank), or that we will never be good enough to find God's love. This message is not biblical, and it can mess up your mind. It is a different type of pornography.

Your spirit must receive truth and refuse to believe these lies. "Father wounds" and other circumstances that happen to us, often early in life, have a stronghold on us that is difficult to overcome. When we grow up feeling unworthy, unwanted, and unloved, it's difficult to accept the fact that we are worthy of God's supremely liberating love. It is through relationships with other believers, reading God's Word, and prayer that we can turn those negative "tapes" that play in our minds over and over to positive messages. That is one powerful benefit of being a Kingsman: surrounding yourself with other people who have traveled down a similar path. We may have been broken and imperfect in the eyes of those around us while growing up, but God created us in His image. We need to remind each other of that life-altering fact.

Refuse to be among the deaf, dumb, and blind. Allow your spirit to awaken your soul.

Building God's Church the Kingsman Way

The Kingsman mentality is based on God's Word. But it is not a list of rules. It is about having a completely different perspective of what it means to have a relationship with a Higher Being. Not rules—a relationship.

One of God's mandates to believers is to "build churches." He is not talking about constructing a facility or planning an event. He wants us to build a relational community in which people grow together spiritually and in every other area of life. Not living in isolation or assuming God will like us better if we do more for Him. It is about joining a family and loving God together. It's about relationships with other believers.

That is why I will continue driving every week at 6:00 a.m. to meet the men who have become my support system, sounding board, and brothers in Christ. Not as a religious duty. But because I have fallen in love with Jesus. Because I am around people who are falling in love with Jesus. Because we are not dead bones, religious legalists, defeated people, or deaf, dumb, or blind. We have found life—real life—through Christ. We are finally hearing, finally speaking, finally seeing truth.

I hope you can join us one day. Become a Kingsman. Enter the family. Wake up from the sleep of religion and see the value of spiritual relationships. Get in your car at 6:00 a.m. Engage in conversations with Jesus and His followers. You—and your life—will never be the same.

CHAPTER
03

Steps on The Journey
of a Kingsman

Let's review the steps from this chapter that will lead you to your ultimate goal of becoming a Kingsman:

1. Join The Kingsman Academy now and surround yourself with the love, support, and kinship of Christian friends and mentors.

2. Build relationships with others to strengthen your relationship with God.

3. Acknowledge any "father wounds" you have been carrying around since childhood. Turn them over to God to begin healing immediately.

4. Recognize that, even if you had a good relationship with your earthly father, it can never come close to the love, protection, guidance, and mercy you will receive from your Heavenly Father.

5. Forgive yourself for your past sins and shortcomings, and recognize that your past or present circumstances do not define who you are. You are a perfect child of God, created in His image. He loves you unconditionally.

6. Understand that as you become a believer and begin walking in the path God has planned for your life, you will experience growing pains. Sometimes you will feel frustration, but your Heavenly Father and fellow believers will support you during the growth process.

7. Stop trying to earn God's love. Jesus paid the ultimate price for our sins when He died on the cross. Just accept this Divine Gift and commit yourself to living within His will.

CHAPTER 04

Our Need for Redemption

Let's return to my 6:00 a.m. adventure. Imagine yourself meeting with a group of people. Your phone alerts you to wake up. Your body resists. Your mind tries to transition from sleeping to being alert. What will you do? Turn off the phone's alarm, and reset it for fifteen more minutes of sleep? Or turn it off, return to sleep, and forget the steps you could take to feed your spiritual hunger?

For now, imagine that you are forcing yourself to get out of bed. You quickly eat, shower, clean up, dress, and get in the car. Turning the keys in the ignition is starting more than just an engine. It is beginning a journey toward growth and development.

Visualize yourself driving and engaging in a conversation with a Father your human eyes cannot see. You are choosing to embrace His acceptance. You are intentionally becoming a Kingsman, experiencing unconditional love and understanding the meaning of undeveloped senses. You are making a rational decision to trust—no matter what emotions lure you away, no matter what thoughts urge you elsewhere. You are being crafted by an Artist who knows you and loves you.

Stopping at a red light, you glance at the mirror. Your face reveals exhaustion, but you see a new energy—like a supernatural power is involved in your life. In the car, you sing songs of worship. Along the way, you pray honest prayers of confession. Nearing your destination, you realize this spiritual adventure of the Kingsman lifestyle is so much more than anything you've ever experienced before.

Redemption Changes Us

To be redeemed means to be saved from sin. It is God's greatest gift to us, and it changes every aspect of our lives in a dramatic way. It's more than a few songs and a short sermon. It's more than legalistic rules and regulations. It is very different from waking up and driving to another prayer meeting to learn a few new points. It is very different from gathering with other people to try to impress one another.

You see it, finally, as what it really is: an adventure. A lifestyle. Someone, after years of conflict and turmoil, grasping unconditional love from his or her Heavenly Father.

You walk into the room with a group of people—people who have made poor decisions in the past, people who have wrestled in the war of religion or relationship, people who need God and one another—who are all different from you but all very similar. You see their faces. You hear their stories. You have entered a spiritual family that has chosen to grasp the truth of redemption.

Now come back to reality. To today. To this moment. What did that imaginary experience feel like? What keeps it from becoming a reality? What steps can you take today to grasp redemption and start on The Journey of a Kingsman?

EACH OF US MUST HAVE A RELATIONSHIP WITH GOD THROUGH JESUS

Let me summarize what it all really means. Each of us must have a relationship with God through Jesus. It happened to me when I totally fell in love with Him. How did that happen? By totally submitting to Him. It was so powerful when I realized there was no real life without Him. It freed me—from condemnation, judgment, and self-hate.

What I am writing here isn't about accomplishments or failures; it is about submitting to God. It is choosing to read God's Word and pray—not being required to read and study but being so madly in love with Him that I want to spend time with Him and His people. I had never had this feeling before, but now I'm starting to understand the basics of living life with God every moment of every day. I sleep with God on my mind. I wake up facing a new day with God on my mind. My newly developed senses are in place because I now have this amazing relationship with Him through Jesus. This is more than reading a book or taking a course. It is getting to know Him personally.

We aren't to be controlled by rules. We are to be guided by our Leader.

When we embrace that concept, we can begin to see school, work, conversations, and worship time from a new perspective. We can absorb truth about redemption together. Thinking together, listening together, learning together, and praying together. Relating to God in school, in sports, in marriage, in family, in all of life. Not letting doctrinal differences divide us but staying true to God's clear message.

This isn't simple for many to grasp. People are so confused. They aren't living with God on a daily basis. They long for their senses to be developed, but they don't know how to make it happen. They are trying so hard to do everything on their own.

If that is you, please don't continue living that way. Embrace God's love, and allow Him to develop your senses by connecting with Him.

Begin with your awareness. Live with an awareness of Him. Live with an awareness that there is more to life. Live with an awareness that in this adventure, your spirit is guiding your decisions.

I am so thankful I have entered this adventure. My only regret is that I waited so long to start. Why didn't I have this relationship before? Legalism kept me away from God. I went to church. I received communion. But I was living like a double agent. Now, I am honored to live as a follower of Christ. I can declare what God has done in my life.

We Must Know God to Know Ourselves

Now that I have been redeemed, I want to tell other people about Jesus. I want you to enter this quest as well.

How we apply our time, resources, and effort is what will ultimately make a difference. Everything has to be about transformation:

- Being able to develop these senses, which helps us understand who God is and who we are.

- Realizing we can't live by feelings.

- Clenching the reality that our spirits are perfect.

We make spiritual life more complicated than it should be. Let's make it relational. Our senses can't be developed if we do not know who God is. That's where it must start. If we don't know who God is, we can't truly

> # IF WE DON'T KNOW WHO GOD IS, WE CAN'T TRULY KNOW WHO WE ARE

know who we are. If we don't know who we are, we can't know what waits for us on the other side. We feel a great sense of being lost.

For the Son of Man came to seek and save those who are lost (Luke 19:10).

Become aware of who God is and who you are. Become aware of what God has done and what you are to do now. It is much more than existing. It is not a secret formula. There are no steps for you to repeat, remember, and rehearse. You need the practicality of living this life with Jesus on a daily basis. That is why this book covers so many areas of life.

And that is why it must start with Jesus.

When we have a personal relationship with Him, He uses our senses to guide our lives. We are connected. He isn't distant. He isn't just a set of rules. He is leading me as a Kingsman each day, each moment, and He can lead you, too.

There was a man named Nicodemus, a Jewish religious leader who was a Pharisee. After dark one evening, he came to speak with Jesus. "Rabbi," he said, "we all know that God has sent you to teach us. Your miraculous signs are evidence that God is with you." Jesus replied, "I tell you the truth, unless you are born again, you cannot see the Kingdom of God" (John 3:1–3).

We Do Not Earn Redemption

Redemption means He saved me. We did not earn redemption; it is His gift to us. When Jesus Christ died on the cross for our sins, He paid the ultimate price for our salvation and thus redemption. That means there is nothing we could ever do to repay Him, so we might as well not even try. We just have to be thankful that it was already done.

But the Holy Spirit produces this kind of fruit in our lives: love, joy, peace, patience, kindness, goodness, faithfulness, gentleness, and self-control. There is no law against these things! (Gal. 5:22–23)

Understand that you were already redeemed. Accept what Christ has done for you. Welcome Jesus into your life. Although that is often viewed as the end, it really is just the beginning. Become part of a spiritual family—those who will encourage you, pray for you, and dare you to become a Kingsman.

We often live in denial of who we really are. We pretend to be people we aren't. End that trend now. Right now! Yes, you've made poor choices, but you are made in God's image. Jesus already paid the full price to cover for your sins. You can now become the person you were created to be. Do not let that tendency inhibit your acceptance. Embrace that truth.

We are nothing without Him. But that is actually good news. We do not need to live this life without Him. Dear friend, grasp that truth. Refuse to let go of it. When thoughts and feelings oppose it, defeat them. Silence them. Delete those files of lies, and welcome the Jesus who has already welcomed you.

Accept God's Love, and Begin to Heal

Tears are pouring down my face as I write this book. I didn't expect it. But I can't help but think about you. Your stories. Your assumptions. Your wounds. Your scars. Why? Because of my own painful account. I have no theological background. I am writing from my wounds, my scars, my personal experience of my own transformation.

And I am thinking about your need for healing.

What does it mean to you to have a relationship with God? What does that look like to you? So many people say they know it, but they really don't. Please do not be one of those people.

For this is how God loved the world: He gave his one and only Son, so that everyone who believes in him will not perish but have eternal life (John 3:16).

Please choose now to accept the love of God. None of these other principles will apply unless you embrace the gift God has given you— the gift of salvation. "Salvation," or "being saved," means that you acknowledge that you are a sinner and that you accept Jesus Christ as your personal Savior. It means that you become a believer, a follower of Christ. It means that you no longer follow the ways of the world but instead live your life in a way that is pleasing to Him.

Becoming a believer is the beginning of a wonderful adventure. It is waking up from a sleep full of nightmares of condemnation and religious effort into a morning of renewal. It is getting in the car and going toward a destination of eternal life while realizing that the ride itself is changing you—and changing the world around you.

I am thinking of you as I write this book. I don't know your story. But please know this: I care about you. I see potential in your life. I am convinced that your spirit can be awakened as you enter The Journey of a Kingsman.

CHAPTER

04

Steps on The Journey of a Kingsman

Let's review the steps from this chapter that will lead you to your ultimate goal of becoming a Kingsman:

1. Expect significant changes in your attitude, views, and mood once you become redeemed, or saved from sin. It will improve every aspect of your life. Join the adventure!

2. Read the Bible, pray, and engage in fellowship with a fellow Kingsman so that you can get to know God more intimately. We must know God to know ourselves.

3. Accept God's love, and begin to heal.

QUEST THREE
SOUL

CHAPTER 05

The Right
Mindset

It's always somebody else's fault.

Unfortunately, too many of us view life that way. Instead of accepting responsibility for things that go wrong, we place blame. Life, for some, is full of excuses. Every bad decision is someone else's fault.

We Must Grow and Become Better Versions of Ourselves

I recently got an opportunity to meet with people from various countries. As I talked to them, I was thinking about the quests in this book: purpose, spirit, soul, body, relationships, family, wealth, contribution, growth, fun, time, and dreams. Their stories reminded me how we often fail to have a positive, responsible mindset in life. So many people frantically work to build their lives, families, and careers, but then everything comes tumbling down. Like a yo-yo, their lives keep going up and down, up and down, up and down. That's what I heard as I listened to the stories of those in this gathering. I didn't hear about steady climbs to the pinnacle of joy, contentment, or success.

So, instead of asking the typical question, "How's everything going?" I probed with deeper questions. I tried to trigger effective responses. I wanted to know why so many people have such a hard time growing. Why so many people stay just where they are. I wanted to hear their thoughts on this theme that is burning in my own heart: "Why are you having such a hard time changing and becoming a better version of yourself?"

A Kingsman Accepts Responsibility

One important hallmark of a Kingsman is taking personal responsibility for our own actions, decisions, and failures. But too many people place blame on others. Very few accept responsibility.

We should all know this by now. There are always excuses. We often

MAKING EXCUSES DISTRACTS US FROM FINDING OUR TRUE PURPOSE

believe one thing didn't work because something else didn't work or someone else didn't make it work. Instead of accepting responsibility, we place blame. Because of a circumstance. Because of a lack of resources. Because of the limited talent around us. There will always be excuses. But making excuses doesn't help us achieve our purpose. It just distracts us from *finding* our true purpose.

For so long, I looked through this same lens: I didn't receive help from a wise mentor. I didn't have enough money. I didn't grow up in the right environment. I didn't live with the right people around me. "Poor me," we think. "I am a victim," we argue. We don't accept responsibility. Instead, we place blame.

What good did that do me? No good. No good at all.

What good will that do you? No good. No good at all.

When we pile excuses on top of excuses, what good do we achieve? The yo-yo effect: we keep bobbing up and down, and eventually we slip backwards. At best, we achieve nothing.

What has changed my own life is choosing to accept responsibility. I call it "having the right mindset."

This can help you better understand what I mean. One person I know well is a hard worker and wants to help others. But he fails to understand the basic life issue of gaining the correct view of spirit, soul, and body. He is frustrated because of what others do or don't do. He has spoken often about how so many people do not accept responsibility, so I started asking him what he believes his true calling in life is. Rather than blaming the world, I wanted him to grasp the truth himself.

We talked about Adam and Eve and the garden: Adam blamed Eve, and Eve blamed the serpent.

"Who told you that you were naked?" the Lord God asked. "Have you eaten from the tree whose fruit I commanded you not to eat?" The man replied, "It was the woman you gave me who gave me the fruit, and I ate it." Then the Lord God asked the woman, "What have you done?" "The serpent deceived me," she replied. "That's why I ate it." (Gen. 3:11–13)

If no one accepts responsibility, no one can move toward freedom. We all need to learn to state this powerful confession: "It's not up to someone else. It is up to me. I accept responsibility."

Think about this. If our spirits come to life as we become new in Christ, we should begin believing what we say we believe. Our spirits are perfect. Our spirits are truly alive. When we finally believe that, when we finally catch up to our true identity in Christ, we no longer blame other people for our faults. In our new spirits, our souls and bodies need to adjust. We develop slowly. It takes time. But that should not keep us from believing the truth and pursuing the destiny God has for us. It begins with awareness. Instead of blaming others and living as victims, we can view ourselves as victors.

Our Spirits Are Already Perfect

Our spirits are already perfect. The first step is becoming fully aware of the fact that our spirits have been made new in Christ. The human soul is a combination of the mind, the will, and the emotions. Our souls are in the process of being renewed. But blaming others causes us to miss opportunities to be transformed. When we accept responsibility, we live with the right mindset, and we can begin to live in the freedom of our new identity in Christ.

Sometimes, we think about how others have wronged us, or we feel negative thoughts about what others have done. We can't help having those thoughts and feelings—or can we? But we definitely should not

THE RIGHT MINDSET PERMITS US TO NOTICE OUR WOUNDS AND SCARS BUT NOT LET THEM DEFINE US

continue to dwell on those things. We shouldn't speak about them constantly. We should see ourselves differently. The right mindset allows us to be aware of past hurts and poor decisions without dwelling on them or blaming others for them. The right mindset permits us to notice our wounds and scars but not let them define us. It inspires us to stand up. It causes us to stop judging ourselves and others. It motivates us to rise above tendencies. It provokes us to see struggles as moments of victory.

With our new mindset, our minds change. We begin to decide what *is* best—not what feels best, not what has always been done, not what others might think is best, but what *is* best. Our emotions might respond quickly or slowly—but they cannot be allowed to control our decisions.

It's not just us. Adam and Eve had the same struggle. To develop the right mindset, we can't blame the snake or the spouse for our willingness to eat the fruit. We admit our own poor decisions and begin to move forward.

Haven't you seen it in your own life? Haven't you seen it in your family? Look at pictures or videos from family gatherings. Replay in your mind conversations from your past. Poor decisions are a part of each of our stories. But they don't have to be the end of our stories. Things can change for the better when we stop placing blame and begin accepting responsibility.

Do not judge others, and you will not be judged. For you will be treated as you treat others. The standard you use in judging is the standard by which you will be judged. And why worry about a speck in your friend's eye when you have a log in your own? (Matt. 7:1–3)

Focus on Your God-Ordained Destiny

When I recently spoke to a group of older people, they clung to my words as I declared what I believe God has planned for me. They were older than me, but I was speaking about a timeless truth of God's purpose for all of us. *Too many people are not living the lives they were designed to be living.* That statement is huge. As my audience listened, they knew they needed to hear that. Each person, no matter how old, needs to gain a better understanding of this truth.

The people in this group were thinking about *survival,* but I wanted them to think about *destiny.* If they could understand that God has a specific purpose for their lives, they could all view their present situations from a better angle.

I wanted them to know the importance of accepting responsibility. I wanted them to adopt the right mindset. I kept telling them to look at what our amazing God does in our lives each day. It is better to think that way than to dwell all day, each day, about the negatives.

One of the things I hear all the time is that people don't fully believe we were all uniquely made for a specific reason. I often ask them to look at the tip of their finger and tell me if there is another one like that in the entire world. I also ask them if there is anyone else in the world who not only looks exactly like them, but also has the same temperament, personality, gifts, talents, and likes. The answer is obviously always no.

Then I go into the fact that if we are all parts of the body, then each and every one of us has to first understand what that is and then become the best part we can be. What I am always trying to get them to understand is that there is a reason they are so frustrated with their lives. I believe they could have been created to be a hand in the body, but they have been acting as a foot their entire lives. Could it kind of work? Sure, but it will never feel right because that's not what they were created to be.

I believe there is a huge journey of self-discovery that most of us never embark on, so we never reach the destiny God has created for us—not because we don't want it, but because we aren't aware of it. All that most people know is that they are extremely frustrated with life, and they have no idea where to start finding their purpose because they don't have a place to plug into where like-minded individuals are constantly seeking the same thing.

Maybe you were not there to hear me that day. But you are reading this right now. Please accept this truth: you were created for a purpose. There is a reason you are here. Until you find that purpose, you will continue to live life as a victim. But when you find that purpose, everything begins to change. We notice the value of our decisions. We notice the potential of our futures. We notice the importance of our present situations. Your mind, will, and emotions are guided by a purpose. So, rather than living as a victim, you live victoriously.

Again, it begins with your mindset. Think about your own life. How would you describe yourself? Are you living with no direction? What inspires you when you wake up in the morning? Who is leading you in this life adventure? Are you a victim or a victor?

Refuse to Let Your Past Control You

What has happened in your life has already happened. There is absolutely nothing you can do to change that. Put an end to being controlled by the past. You don't have to start over. You just have to start again.

When I was seventeen, I had already moved from Brazil to America by myself. I was working and making money, hoping to make a difference in this life. Looking back, I know God was preparing me to learn my true calling, my true purpose. As I see people now in their twenties and thirties with no awareness of their destiny, I shudder. Whatever brought them to these circumstances? They live at their parents' homes, they have no jobs, and they have no apparent purpose. I see the victim perspective in their minds. Bound by this blame-shifting, they are left with no direction, no inspiration. And this generation is left with no world-changers. Many of them have already given up. They are victims when they should be victors.

I am thinking about the privilege of being a Kingsman. That is how we should view ourselves. What if those older people I spoke to had been exposed to this truth earlier in life? How much pain could they have avoided? How many poor decisions would they have avoided?

Imagine what their lives could have been like, had they been able to develop this level of thinking early on in life—imagine where they would be right now. What businesses would they be leading? What temptations would they be resisting?

What if the younger people I speak to on a daily basis will now receive this truth? How much pain can they avoid? How many great decisions can they make?

What about you? What about your mind, will, and emotions? What about your past, your present, your future?

And now, just as you accepted Christ Jesus as your Lord, you must continue to follow him. Let your roots grow down into him, and let your lives be built on him. Then your faith will grow strong in the truth you were taught, and you will overflow with thankfulness (Col. 2:6–7).

Remember, what happens is not somebody else's fault or responsibility. It is yours. It is mine. It is ours.

CHAPTER

05

Steps on The Journey
of a Kingsman

Let's review the steps from this chapter that will lead you to your ultimate goal of becoming a Kingsman:

1. Accept responsibility for your actions and attitude to grow and become a better version of yourself, which will honor God.

2. Focus on your God-ordained destiny.

3. Refuse to let your past control you or hold you back from the phenomenal success and happiness God wants you to have.

4. Don't start over; just start again—on the right path.

CHAPTER 06

From Victim to Victor

"Are you sure your son is only nine?"

A friend asked me that question when he noticed my son's attitude and maturity. Though only nine, having the right mindset is influencing a young boy.

Think about how it can influence you. Think about how you can then influence many others.

No matter your age. No matter your life stories. Instead of placing blame, you can accept responsibility. Instead of living as a victim, you can live victoriously.

In Chapter 5, I talked about taking responsibility for our own decisions, circumstances, and lives. Here we'll go deeper into that concept. This can change your life, my friend. If you choose to accept this new perspective, your life will never be the same.

I strongly contend that young people should have a clear direction of where God wants them to go. It seems that few do. Why is that the exception? Why can't it be the norm?

We keep allowing ourselves to get stuck in the victim mentality. As long as we do this, we will never be able to move forward. When that

> ## WE KEEP ALLOWING OURSELVES TO GET STUCK IN THE VICTIM MENTALITY

bleeds into our mindset about discipleship, we overcomplicate it. But when it's done well, it can put people into the victor mentality. God has a perfect plan in place for every one of us. All we need to do is step into it and follow. We are called to do it as a part of the large group of disciples of Christ. You are called to be a disciple and to disciple others.

Teaching Our Children to Be Victors

We should talk to our kids regularly about this; they will get it. When we talk about God, about the fact that He created them, about their purpose, about being victors instead of victims, our young people can begin grasping real ways to fulfill God's plan for their lives.

Recently, I talked to my son, Matthew about this. He is nine, but talking to him is like talking to someone my own age. It's the coolest thing.

Most parents tend to see situations like their children battling stress and think something is wrong. Some parents even use medication to calm their children. I see in my son's struggles something positive that just needs to be channeled the right way. Things will go wrong in our lives, regardless of how young or old we are. When our children suffer disappointments, that is our cue to teach them about how to find solutions, maintain a positive attitude anyway, and move past the setbacks. Teaching children to turn to God in times of hardship is one of the most valuable gifts we can give them.

Matthew looks just like me, and he is a lot like me. I see in him the potential to be much more grounded in purpose than I was at his age. I want to offer him more than medication to get through the challenges of life. I want him to know that he is a child of God and that he can turn to God during his times of need.

To help Matthew learn and reach his God-given purpose, I talked to a friend who is a performance coach. He helps people deal with trauma, unlocking their true potential and moving toward reaching their destiny. He told Matthew that the reason he was having certain challenges in his life that could not be explained is because his mind had some type of "error message" that was caused by a past trauma. He encouraged

Matthew to spend a couple of hours going through mental exercises to clear those error messages and allow his mind to heal itself.

The Past Does Not Define Us

Often, our minds act as if past traumas are still occurring. Past pain is real in the present. My friend helps people realize the fact that past traumas do not control their present lives. When people talk about stories from their past, they often feel defeated, as if that situation defines who they are now. But with the right mindset, they can talk about the story but no longer be controlled by it.

If we want different results, we need to do something different. Pretty obvious, right?

My wife and I both went through the process my friend created. We wanted to unlock our true potential but were unable to do it on our own. We didn't want to be controlled by the past. We were looking at each other, asking, "What happened to us?" We didn't want to be victims. We wanted to be victorious.

The process helped us. And I knew it could help my son as well.

When Matthew walked out from his session, it looked like a hundred pounds had been lifted off his shoulders. He had a huge smile on his face. I thought, "Wow, this is amazing."

The coolest thing, though, is what happened on the way there. I was talking to him about purpose and college and his destiny. He said, "I want to do something I love for the rest of my life. I don't want to just work for the money and be stuck doing something I wasn't created to do."

Even though I had been teaching Matthew these things since he was four years old, I love hearing him talk about it. We talked about people who went to law school but weren't working as lawyers, those who went to medical school but weren't working as doctors, and those who went to engineering school but weren't working as engineers.

"Why would somebody go to school for that many years if they weren't one hundred percent sure that is what they wanted to do for the rest of their lives?" he asked.

He continued thinking and asking questions. "If you go to school for something, shouldn't you be sure that is what you want to do for the rest of your life?"

He's only nine, but he gets it. Aren't we all supposed to be doing something we love, something we are good at? I kept saying, "Yes! That's how it's supposed to be."

We Must Discover and Live Our True Purpose

Then, imagine how I felt when my son told me this: "You have no idea how much I appreciate having you in my life."

I asked, "Why?"

He said, "I talk to my friends, and they don't have what we have. Just like what we are doing now. They don't have conversations like this with their dads."

Those are the words of a nine-year-old. He sees how, as is often said, "hurt people hurt people." He is already noticing how those with victim mentalities cannot move forward. They miss out on healthy relationships. Their souls aren't in the process of healing. They remain in pain because they aren't actively pursuing healing. They can't reach their potential because they refuse to grasp the wisdom of a child who is driven by purpose.

"Thank you for being such a good mentor," my son told me.

Do I feel like a good mentor? No. Do my mind, will, and emotions always grasp the full truth of God's plan for me? No. But I choose to believe this is my calling, my purpose.

Life isn't supposed to be a series of events that always end up hurting people.

Let's stop making excuses. Let's refuse to be victims.

Maybe you think my son is too young to know the types of struggles life can bring. But he knows life isn't always easy, despite his young age. Matthew was born at twenty-nine weeks, weighing only three pounds and nine ounces. He has been through eight surgeries. The doctor told us he would never be able to talk or walk.

Later that day, I told my wife what Matthew said to me. I said, "Hearing Matthew say that to me reminded me again of my true purpose. I can make a positive difference in his life, knowing that he will make a huge difference in the lives of so many others."

Too many people wait too long to grasp this. Too many of us wander through the proverbial desert for forty years. Matthew is getting through that same desert in twelve days. And we can, too! But unless there is a constant renewing of our minds, we will stay in the desert. God wants to renew you, to speak into your life as your Father, even when your earthly dad does not encourage you. God can. God will.

Are you listening? He is telling you your value, your importance, your purpose. He is guiding you from being a victim to being a victor.

I love the way my son thinks. Shouldn't we all think that way?

Step Out into the Unknown by Faith

But how? How can we do this? First, we must become aware of this: we need to step out by faith.

Faith shows the reality of what we hope for; it is the evidence of things we cannot see (Heb. 11:1).

God wants you to have an amazing life. But unless you step by faith into the unknown, you will miss the opportunity. Without faith, you won't be a victorious, purposeful person. Too many of us live as victims, controlled by whatever happens to us, rather than seeing life through the eyes of faith.

Are you realizing who you really are? Have you accepted Jesus as your Lord and Savior? Do you realize you are a child of God?

Become aware that you are a victor already. The process isn't always quick or simple. But you must engage in this adventure with the right perspective: you are already a victor! Decide to live with the basic awareness that your spirit is holy, clean, pure, and perfect.

When you think about something, it becomes an emotion, and your will takes action. You cannot get where God wants you to go unless you change the way you think. Your soul will learn to respond victoriously as it is renewed.

The process of getting that truth to your soul and body happens as you renew your mind daily, as you change the way you think.

We all want to live a good, pleasing, and perfect life. We think; we feel; we act. But we must decide *how* to think and act. We can reach our potential by having the right view. How do we obtain that victorious view?

- Realize what we have and who we are.
- Admit what is standing in the way (e.g., pride, blame, fear).
- Unlock and overcome it.
- Pursue our destiny.

Isn't that the adventure you want to experience? Think about how it can change your life—your present and your future. Think about how it can keep you from being controlled by your past. Changing your perspective from victim to victor can radically change your life. Will you let it?

Make Wise Choices Consciously

We often think that because we are making choices on a daily basis, we have full control. But choices are nothing but an illusion. What you are truly making are superficial decisions. Every decision you make is

CHOICES ARE NOTHING BUT AN ILLUSION

based on information you already had. Your subconscious mind is really making the choices for you.

Even though we don't want to do something because we know we shouldn't, we do it anyway. Have you ever wondered why? You are a product of your environment, and unless you decide to change and consciously start making actual choices, the repetitive pattern you have been exposed to your entire life will choose for you. Living any other way will never give you the real freedom to choose.

Think about this: If you were hungry and had the option to "choose" between the type of food you have been eating your entire life—and let's assume it's not the healthiest option—and food that would be completely different but healthier, which would you choose? You want to think you would choose the healthy one because you know for a fact it is good for you. But the reality is that when the opportunity presents itself, you will very likely go back to what you are used to. Why? Because you have been trained to make that choice your entire life. You can't help yourself. Keep this in mind: whatever you digest becomes a part of who you are.

What have you been feeding your thoughts with? Do you think it is time for a change?

God created the world in steps. He likes order. He likes things organized. He likes simple things people can follow. Things that make our lives simpler.

Follow these simple steps:

- Accept Jesus as your personal Savior.
- Embrace your new spirit.
- Begin to develop your soul by renewing your mind.

Your body will start looking different because of the new decisions you are going to make moving forward. That is God's order. That is what we can follow. That is how we reach our potential. This is how He lays it out. To remind yourself of God's plea that we become new people in Him, I recommend that you read and process Romans 12:2 often:

> *Don't copy the behavior and customs of this world, but let God transform you into a new person by changing the way you think. Then you will learn to know God's will for you, which is good and pleasing and perfect (Rom. 12:2).*

Remember, it all goes back to the way you think. Beginning now, you must no longer see yourself as a victim. You must—today—see yourself as a victor. This often requires a conscious change in your mindset.

CHAPTER

06

Steps on The Journey
of a Kingsman

Let's review the steps from this chapter that will lead you to your ultimate goal of becoming a Kingsman:

1. Lose the victim mentality; picture yourself as a victor instead of a victim.

2. Teach your children to be victors.

3. Discover and live your true (God-given) purpose.

4. Step out into the unknown by faith.

5. Make wise choices consciously.

QUEST FOUR
BODY

CHAPTER 07

The Outer You

In my search for meaning, I realized that unless I was willing to give my body as a living sacrifice, I would never be able to claim the rewarding life God had in store for me.

My mind and emotions had taken a huge hit after certain experiences I had that, to say the least, would make anyone who had a better understanding about God's purpose for our life here on this Earth question himself. The Bible tells us to love God above all things and to love our neighbors as ourselves. These are the two greatest commandments. But what happens when you don't love yourself, and your neighbor has done so much against you that thinking about the experience causes you the biggest pain you have ever felt deep down in your soul? That kind of experience takes a toll on your spirit, your soul, and your body—the outer you.

Eating Myself to Death

A few years ago, my wife and I started a competition to see which one of us could transform his or her body faster in a period of ninety days. We not only signed up for gym memberships and invested heavily in new eating habits; we also hired two personal trainers who would guide us each step of the way to achieve the results we were looking for. We documented the entire process in a YouTube channel I created called "Um Brasileiro Na América." In this channel, we shared our experiences in the United States with our fellow Brazilians, hoping to inspire them to follow their dreams and perhaps choose to also change their lives.

Three months later, having lost twelve pounds, Daniela won the competition. I was almost as successful, having lost ten pounds. Energized by our success, we continued to eat healthy foods and work out for a few more months. Then we started to slip back into our old, bad habits, probably because we did what most people do. We thought we could keep achieving higher results on our own. It wasn't until later that we fully understood the real power that mentorship had given us throughout this entire process.

"What happened to all that drive and motivation?" I kept asking myself. As I looked in the mirror, I couldn't help but feel extremely sorry for myself—like a true victim of my circumstances. I had gained forty pounds in a few short months. I felt ashamed of myself. My cheeks were puffy, I had a double chin, and my breathing was heavy. My button-down shirts seemed like they were going to explode. I had to wear a sweater on top of them, and I couldn't get my pants on past my thighs. I felt horrible.

"This isn't me," I told myself every time I reached for clothes that no longer fit. I had been literally eating myself to death for months, hoping that all the food would somehow take the pain away—or at least numb it, even for a brief moment.

With a clouded mind and no motivation to keep moving forward, I once again got down on my knees and asked for help. "What do You want me to do?" I asked God. "I can't do this on my own." I could feel His presence. I knew then what He wanted me to do.

A Forty-Day Fast Renews My Physical and Spiritual Strength

He inspired me to start an incredible forty-day journey of healing—not because I needed to do it to please Him, but so He could once again bring healing to my life.

And so, dear brothers and sisters, I plead with you to give your bodies to God because of all he has done for you. Let them be a living and holy sacrifice—the kind he will find acceptable. This is truly the way to worship him (Rom. 12:1).

During those forty days, I would eat no food. I hoped the fast would give me the clarity I needed to start on this new journey I was about to embark on of getting rid of all the junk in my life—food—that was cluttering my system and mind and keeping me from processing information like I should.

Matthew 4:1–11 tells the important story of how the Holy Spirit led Jesus into the wilderness to fast for forty days and nights. This fast immediately followed Jesus's baptism (Matt. 3:13), which began his public ministry. While Jesus was fasting, the devil repeatedly tempted him.

Why would God test his only son, whom he loved, like this? He did it to prepare Jesus for the three-year ministry that would change the entire world forever.

As Jesus became weaker, Satan took advantage of the situation. He tempted Jesus to give in to His natural desires and attacked His identity as the Son of God. Each time Satan tempted Jesus, He recited the Word of God to resist him. He didn't rely on His own strength (human at that time) to resist temptation and refrain from sinning. This is a critical lesson for you as a Kingsman: fasting can boost our spiritual strength and bring us closer to God.

Then Jesus was led by the Spirit into the wilderness to be tempted there by the devil. For forty days and forty nights he fasted and became very hungry. During that time the devil came and said to him, "If you are the Son of God, tell these stones to become loaves of bread." But Jesus told him, "No! The Scriptures say, 'People do not live by bread alone, but by every word that comes from the mouth of God.'" Then the devil took him to the holy city, Jerusalem, to the highest point of the Temple, and said, "If you are the Son of God, jump off! For the Scriptures say, 'He will order his angels to protect you. And they will hold you up with their hands so you won't even hurt your foot on a stone.'" Jesus responded, "The Scriptures also say, 'You must not test the Lord your God.'" Next the devil took him to the peak of a very high mountain and showed him all the kingdoms of the world and their glory. "I will give it all to you," he said, "if you will kneel down and worship me." "Get out of here, Satan," Jesus told him. "For the Scriptures say, 'You must worship the Lord your God and serve only him.'" Then the devil went away, and angels came and took care of Jesus (Matt 4:1–11).

Was this easy for Jesus? No. For me? Not at all—but absolutely worth it.

As each day went by, I realized how much of an impact something as simple—and to a certain extent harmless—as food has, not only on my body, but also on my mind. The clarity that came from that experience was simply amazing. It might seem that without food, the body and mind would grow weaker, but I experienced just the opposite. As each day

> # AS EACH DAY WENT BY, I GREW STRONGER, AND MY MIND GREW SHARPER

went by, I grew stronger, and my mind grew sharper. I started seeing things in a way I had never been able to see before.

Recognize Your Value

Imagine waking up on a stunning Saturday morning. Everyone else is still asleep as the sunrise greets you with a smile. A few clouds glance back at you, inviting you to celebrate the weekend. You smell the coffee brewing, and you can almost taste it before you take your first sip. You pour the cup full.

Suddenly, your doorbell rings. You reach over to snatch the coffee, almost tripping on the carpet as you walk toward the front door. You aren't expecting company.

Opening the door surprises you again. No one is there. You look around, feeling a nice, gentle breeze in the air but seeing no one. You take another sip of coffee and notice a note lying on the porch, with a key.

The note tells you to glance toward the left of your driveway to see a gift that has been left there for you. You look in that direction, shocked to see a Ferrari shining with beauty, reflecting the morning sun.

Your name is on that note. It says, "This is my gift to you. Take care of it for the rest of your life. Enjoy it. Love, Dad."

What words would you use to describe that moment? What phrases would reveal how you feel as you see that Ferrari? How do you think others would feel if they saw you driving it?

Think about this. From the moment you are born, your body is like that brand-new Ferrari you have just been given. Throughout your life, you're going to have the option to keep it inside the house and take it for a spin only occasionally. You're going to have a choice to fuel it with the cheapest or the most expensive fuel available. You're going to have a chance to follow the scheduled maintenance suggested by the manufacturer. You're going to have a chance to keep it clean. You're going to have a chance to keep that Ferrari looking beautiful and performing well.

Like any exotic car, this Ferrari didn't come with a cheap price tag. Why do you believe it costs so much? I will tell you why—the manufacturer took a long time to make it. Each one is unique.

The difference is that, unlike the Ferrari, God made only one of you. You were uniquely made. Your fingerprint is the only one like it in the entire world. Please understand that God distinctively crafted and designed you for a purpose. He has a mesmerizing plan for you. Even though we've all failed, and we carry the history of sin from the Garden of Eden, where Adam and Eve ate the fruit God forbade them to eat, God has purchased us again.

You are worth a lot more than that Ferrari. You are way more important, way more valuable.

Take Good Care of Your Physical Health

We are all given something phenomenal when we are born—more than the perfect car that looks simply incredible. We have everything we will ever need. The problem is that as we age, we feel and look more like a beaten-up old Beetle than a classic Ferrari.

Why is that? Because we intentionally want to harm our bodies? No! Mainly because we have this amazing vehicle, but we have no idea how to take care of it. We put in cheap gas (junk food), rarely ever take it for a ride (exercise), and don't ever do the scheduled maintenance (preventive care) like we should. We react, only checking things out when something is going wrong—which is usually a little too late.

Why? Why do we do what we shouldn't? And why don't we do what we should? Often because we just don't know what to do. We allow our emotions to dictate how much we eat and how much we sit around and do nothing. We are also influenced by our environment, so if our family and friends eat only bad food, we feel we would be disconnected if we didn't join them. The decisions we make on a daily basis dictate how we live and what our health looks like. We are products of our environment, but we can do something about this. We can learn more and live better as we begin to understand how much we are truly worth.

Imagine for a moment that the average life span is 120 years, which would be more likely to occur if we were correctly taking care of our bodies. If that Ferrari was worth $300,000 today and you took very good care of it, what do you think it would be worth 120 years from now? The same amount you paid? No. It will be worth millions of dollars. Why? Because it would now be a classic car, right? It is not only a classic, but it is 120 years old. It has also been so well taken care of that it can function just like it functioned when you first purchased it.

We've all been given more than a Ferrari. Let's accept ourselves. Let's *value* ourselves. That view can bring positive changes into our lives.

Don't you realize that your body is the temple of the Holy Spirit, who lives in you and was given to you by God? You do not belong to yourself (1 Cor. 6:19).

Your Body Is a Reflection of Your Values

Your body is God's temple. That is where the Holy Spirit lives. The question is, are you showing due respect for the dwelling place of God's Spirit?

WHAT DOES YOUR APPEARANCE SAY ABOUT YOUR SPIRIT?

What does your body—your outer you—say about your beliefs? What does your appearance say about your spirit? What does that first impression reveal about God?

What do you think is going through my mind when I look into doing business with a person who is severely overweight, not because of a disease, but because he is always eating unhealthy food? I'd be thinking, "If that is the lack of discipline he has with his body, imagine the type of discipline he must have in business."

Of course, those initial thoughts are not always true. Carrying extra weight and having major health issues could be caused by other conditions, not to mention past traumas and emotional issues. But I am talking about first impressions. If that thought crosses my mind, it could potentially influence me the wrong way. Right or wrong, that is reality. Do not deny that. Accept it. And think about what that means to you—

and your view of your physical well-being. Realize that it is OK to seek help to become healthier and stronger.

The Kingsman mentality isn't just someone saying, "I'm trying to eat better. I'm trying to do more for my health." We know that how we view ourselves influences how we treat ourselves and that how others view us influences how they treat us.

There Is No Such Thing as "Trying"

I once heard performance coach Tony Robbins tell a story about a person who said he was "trying" to do something. Tony threw a chair on the floor and said, "Would you try to pick up that chair?" When the person picked up the chair, Robbins said, "What are you doing?"

"I'm picking up the chair."

"No, I didn't tell you to *pick* up the chair," Robbins said. "I told you to *try* to pick up the chair."

The person was confused and just stood there, looking at Robbins.

"Aren't you going to try to pick up the chair?" Robbins asked.

"Well, I did. But you told me not to."

"No, you weren't *trying.* You picked up the chair, and now you're just not picking it up."

Robbins was making the point that "trying to do something" doesn't exist; you either do it or you don't do it.

The same is true with our bodies. Many people live a life of excuses, of reasons it won't work for them. But as a Kingsman, you must always remember: your body belongs to God.

Again, please do not let these words sound judgmental. I know it isn't always easy. We have all struggled in this area. I certainly have. But as I explained earlier, you need to choose to live in a new environment. You need to think differently because you are a Kingsman now. We all have different reasons, better reasons, deeper reasons to care for ourselves. Not selfish reasons, but holy reasons. God-directed reasons. Our whole purpose is different from that of those who don't see life the way we see it.

Identify the Problem, and Choose to Fix It

When you know deep inside that your body is not the ideal reflection of God's handiwork, you can take three steps to correct the situation:

- Become aware there is an issue.
- Determine what the issue is.
- Decide to do something about it.

The first step is to *become aware there is an issue*. Many people grow up not eating healthy diets. Maybe their meals were high in carbs or low in protein. As products of our environments, we become unhealthy, like our diets. But do we have to stay there for the rest of our lives? No. We can change it.

You can change your story. Not by chance; it happens by choice. There are steps to take, goals to set, plans to make. There is a second step: *determine what the issue is*. Don't just notice something is wrong. Find ways to determine the cause. Talk to a doctor, research your family's medical history, and identify poor habits. These are just a few of the steps you can follow to determine the deep, true issues.

After becoming aware there is an issue and determining what the issue is, the third step is to decide to do something about it. *Find a way to fix the issue.*

Here is how you find out if you really want to do something about it. You might say, "I want to go to the gym every day." But if you don't go to the gym every day, do you really want to? I think you know the answer. It isn't *wanting* to do something or *trying* to do something—it is really doing it!

Please do not tell yourself you don't have time. There is one thing every person has: time. Look at a single father who works two jobs and is successful at home and on the job. Would you be shocked to see him with a fit body? If he's in shape, that means this: he finds time to keep his body healthy. He has the same twenty-four hours as other people and more responsibilities than many others. But he *chooses* to work out. He *chooses* to eat better. He *chooses* to view his body as a gift from God, something to value and treat correctly. I want to learn from his dedication. I want us all to learn from him.

Managing time comes from a conscious decision. Those who seriously want a healthier body and a better life find a way to solve any problem standing in their way to achieving that goal.

Look in the mirror. You can't see your soul or your spirit. What do you see? Your body. What is the present condition of the body you see? Are you overweight? Do you have little energy? Have you attempted quick fixes for your health instead of long-term solutions for your physical well-being? Are you loading up on coffee all day? What pills are you taking? Are you relying on alcohol to deaden your pain?

Let the answers to those questions be signs about how you view your body. Do you see your body as God wants you to see it? He sees you as important. He sees you as His child. He sees you as a Kingsman. Begin to see yourself that way. And let the view you have of yourself inspire you to take care of your body.

Change your view of yourself. Change your relationship with food and your body. Set clear goals that are appealing. Be disciplined. You will be thankful for making these decisions.

Focus on your sleep for a moment. If your body needs eight hours of sleep but you are only getting six, where do you think those other two hours will come from? Your body needs that energy. When that happens, many people choose to position external things into their bodies for a false sense of energy.

These are the questions I want you to ask yourself: Are you aware of your physical condition? Are you determined to do something about it? Are you willing to find a solution and stick with it?

Make Long-Term Changes in Your Attitude and Lifestyle

As you commit to transforming your outer you, think about what steps to take. Don't pursue quick, temporary fixes. We are talking about lifestyle changes. Energy drinks aren't the answer. Fad diets aren't the

> # DON'T PURSUE QUICK, TEMPORARY FIXES

key. Think of long-term solutions. Eat right. Get enough sleep. Exercise. Let's not make this too complicated.

Instead of a fad, this requires a change of perspective about ourselves and our bodies, as well as a change in lifestyle. Be a life student regarding your health. Your body needs a lifetime of care.

All twelve of these quests work together; we should seek to master them. My intention here is not to give you a step-by-step meal plan or a one-month exercise plan. Other books can do that. This book dares you to grasp the Kingsman mindset. Implementation comes when we grasp the larger picture—who we are, why we are important, and how we respond to that knowledge.

Something that is in motion tends to stay in motion. Something static tends to stay that way. A car that is not moving cannot be steered. Choose to be a body in motion.

Everyone is created differently. The way your body responds will be unique to you. So, aside from weight, height, or appearance, we are dared to value our bodies correctly.

Go back to the beginning. Imagine what Adam and Eve looked like. What did their chests, their arms, and their legs look like? God created them with the exact amount of muscle, height, and fat they needed.

So God created human beings in his own image. In the image of God he created them; male and female he created them (Gen. 1:27).

Let Your Uniqueness Inspire You

We are all different. Taller, shorter. Faster, slower. Born into a family with more weight or more height. Don't let that discourage you. Let it inspire you to acquire knowledge, and then to action. Based on your own personality and physique, on your family history and design, what is the best version of you that you can be? Think about your uniqueness while also grasping this thrilling call from God to value and treat yourself correctly.

Live intentionally. It is a process but can be done. Not in your own strength but by the power of the Holy Spirit. Become a student of the Kingsman perspective. Learn why you overeat and refuse to exercise. Based on your unique characteristics, what should your body fat be like? What type of exercise is best for you? What is the level of thinking that has caused you to make the decisions you've made up until this point?

Has your relationship with food taken the place of your relationship with God? Which of these quests have you ignored, and how could that have caused you to view your physical well-being incorrectly or worse yet, completely neglect it?

Ask yourself those questions. As you answer them, remember that God is there with you to remind you of His love. Live knowing that the outer you can be a healthy display of the Kingsman spirit within you.

CHAPTER

07

Steps on The Journey
of a Kingsman

Let's review the steps from this chapter that will lead you to your ultimate goal of becoming a Kingsman:

1. Consider fasting to renew your physical strength.

2. Recognize your value.

3. Take good care of your body. It is God's temple.

4. There is no such thing as trying; just do it.

5. Identify the problem, and choose to fix it.

6. Make long-term changes in your attitude and lifestyle.

7. Let your uniqueness inspire you.

QUEST FIVE

RELATIONSHIPS

CHAPTER 08

The Power of
Mentorship

My hope is that, after going through four of the twelve quests, you have come to realize that each one of the quests is unique yet vital if you are serious about reaching your true potential. And although they are all unique, I also hope you realize by now that they all have one very important theme in common: relationships.

Relationships Are Vital to Our Well-Being

Relationships are fundamental to every part of the Kingsman journey, including your purpose, spirit, soul, wealth, growth, and time. If I could narrow down my story and lessons to one all-inclusive, all-important word, "relationships" is it.

EVERY AREA OF LIFE IS INFLUENCED BY RELATIONSHIPS

Every area of life is influenced by relationships.

Pain from past relationships can cause us to avoid future relationships and impact how we perceive people in the present. Think about churches and jobs. Think about business endeavors and athletic teams. Think about family reunions and family division. Think about arguments, conflict on the job, bitterness, and rude comments. Think about how counseling sessions lure clients toward finally facing how they have been hurt by someone, somewhere, at some time. They all connect us in some way to relationships.

We see important relationships in the Bible. We see them through history. We see them in our own quests. People beside people. Hurting people beside hurting people. Performance, competition, division, wounds.

But there can be so much more to relationships. There can be positive, life-changing, eternity-altering outcomes to healthy relationships.

Yes, I know about the pain that relationships can bring. The next chapter will really drive this point home because I will be exposing some of my deepest wounds. My main goal is to help you understand that this is all part of an ongoing training that addresses these issues so that we can find healthy methods of moving past the pain.

In the next few chapters, I also discuss a topic that most people are uncomfortable with— money—and the issues that most people face because of the lack of training and instruction about handling their finances. You may not realize it, but money is one of the biggest issues to arise in relationships. The truth is that most of us have never been taught how to develop healthy relationships. Everyone is so busy chasing their own tails that few pursue true, meaningful relationships. We simply don't take the time to learn how this single most important aspect of life is supposed to be handled.

But we must. We must take time—make time—to develop the right relationships that will support us along our journey. We need to be mentored by someone who has been there before us, and we must be willing to invest the time to mentor others the first opportunity we get. This is the Kingsman mindset.

One day as Jesus was walking along the shore of the Sea of Galilee, he saw two brothers—Simon, also called Peter, and Andrew—throwing a net into the water, for they fished for a living. Jesus called out to them, "Come, follow me, and I will show you how to fish for people!" And they left their nets at once and followed him. (Matt. 4:18–20).

God Brought a Mentor to Me Who Saved My Life

Fortunately, I have been honored to meet a man who taught me about true mentorship. Through Larry, I learned the positive side of relationships. You've already read about how he impacted my life in a positive way. But the fact is, you don't quite understand the whole picture yet. I want to tell you more about it in this chapter because I had the privilege of learning from Larry what true leaders do, and most importantly, how they treat others.

What made the experience I had with Larry so different from anything I had ever experienced in my life up until that point?

Was it because he is a well-known pastor? No, that wasn't it.

Was it because he is an international speaker who leads a fantastic ministry, used by God all over the world to impact lives like mine? No, that wasn't it.

Was it because I was impressed to see that he doesn't think like most pastors I had met over the years who believe that, because they are supported by churches and ministries, they cannot live in a nice home, drive good cars, or have an abundant and prosperous life all around? No, that wasn't it.

Was it because he opened the doors to his home and took me in for a whole month after meeting me only once, so he could get to know me and teach me the one simple concept I had had such a hard time dealing with all my life—receiving—without expecting anything in return? No, that wasn't it.

The reason Larry got to me was because he was willing to simply love me. He wanted to have a relationship with me without an agenda. Nothing else. Absolutely nothing else. He wasn't trying to prove that he was something great. He wasn't displaying his talent. He wasn't performing and growing his platform. He was just being himself.

He taught me how to deal with what I was going through. He simply told me what he had gone through in the past, that people had called him names and turned against him. By doing so, he helped me relate to my pain. He listened. He cared. He took time to be there for me. He shared with me that, like me, he had also built something amazing some time back but was wrongfully accused of doing something he wouldn't ever be able to do, even in his wildest dreams. He also shared how all the good he had accomplished in his lifetime of work was suddenly completely damaged because someone decided they wanted to do something they shouldn't.

What did he do about it? He endured the pain and continued to care for people. I could relate to his story. After enduring so much pain and having so many people turning against me, I decided to leave the city I had been living in for the previous nine years and give up on everything I had built up until that point. When I did so, he was there, mentoring me toward healing. Yes, I was bitter, but I learned how to avoid caring too much about what people do to me, how they treat me, or even how they think about me. I learned that the best investment I can make is in people. If I decided to go through life bitter and avoid relationships because at one point people are going to hurt me again—which is a fact—then what would be the point of living?

Please understand that. This is huge. This changed my life. I quickly realized that if God created me to have a vertical relationship with Him, but I am not willing to develop horizontal relationships with others, I am missing His ultimate calling for my life. After all, didn't Jesus say that the two greatest commandments are to love God above all things and love our neighbor as ourselves? So with that, if I don't care for those around me, I am not truly obeying Him, am I?

Do you understand how rare this type of mentoring is in our culture?

Larry came into my life unexpectedly. But it wasn't a coincidence. God put him in my path at the exact moment I needed him. And He will do the same for you. Be open to finding the mentor who will change—and maybe even save—your life.

God Created Us to Be in Relationships

I wasted so much time in the first four years I lived in the United States. I was too busy and too focused on myself to grasp and pursue a mentor or even just develop relationships.

What about you? Who is your mentor? Do you have one?

It's hard to stay in touch with everyone consistently, we say. But is building and maintaining healthy relationships as difficult as we really think?

God created us to be in relationships. Not having relationships nearly cost me my life. The enemy, Satan, wants you to be alone—that's how he gets to you.

Why do so few people ever have a mentor? Because it's hard. Very few people are like Larry—willing to pour their wisdom, time, and care into someone's life.

Direct mentors are crucial to our success in life. Those who drive for thirty minutes early in the morning to meet together. Those who ask us deep questions, seeking honest answers. My face-to-face time with Larry was essential to my growth.

If you don't have access to someone like Larry today, don't allow that to stop you from growing and moving forward. We live in the best day and age in the history of the world. Because of technology, we can learn from all types of experts and leaders through their books, seminars, and podcasts. This is a way, even if indirect, to bring mentors into your life. I did that for years, and you can do it, too. As a matter of fact, if you'll allow me, I would love to be that resource for you. I would love to be able to guide you on this journey. This book is just the beginning. I would love to be able to connect with you, stay in touch with you, and be a part of your growth—of your own journey toward being a true Kingsman. To warn you about the obstacles, to caution you. To go through these twelve quests with you. Your perspective, your habits, your relationships, and your life will be changed forever. Becoming a Kingsman is only the first step in this amazing journey of healing, empowerment, and true lasting transformation.

We must invest in people—always. We should never do anything on our own. Be a mentor to your children and spouse first, but find someone else you can mentor. I am not talking about fake Facebook friends. It's not about quantity; it is about quality.

Why So Few People Have Mentoring Relationships

So, if mentoring is so important, why do so many people have so few—if any—mentors? Again, it isn't easy. Relationships sometimes bring hurt, disagreement, and failures. Mistakes come with relationships. That is why love and forgiveness are key in the power of mentorship.

The three most common reasons people give me for not mentoring or being mentored by someone are the pain they've experienced in past relationships, a lack of commitment to invest the work to make mentoring happen, and a lack of time. People say, "I can't fit any more responsibilities into my schedule" and "If only I had forty-eight hours in a day."

It amazes me how much time is wasted because of the limiting beliefs we have. What kind of relationships do you currently have? As I've already mentioned several times, everything boils down to relationships—with our time, wealth, bodies, and the other nine quests through *The Journey of a Kingsman*. You must master relationships, or you will end up going through life bitter and alone. Face it: no matter how much you try to ignore your need for relationships, it will always be there.

All the believers devoted themselves to the apostles' teaching, and to fellowship, and to sharing in meals (including the Lord's Supper), and to prayer. A deep sense of awe came over them all, and the apostles performed many miraculous signs and wonders. And all the believers met together in one place and shared everything they had. They sold their property and possessions and shared the money with those in need. They worshiped together at the Temple each day, met in homes for the Lord's Supper, and shared their meals with great joy and generosity— all the while praising God and enjoying the goodwill of all the people. And each day the Lord added to their fellowship those who were being saved. (Acts 2:42–47).

Jesus Was the Ultimate Mentor

If you could pick one of the key roles Jesus fulfilled, what would it be? To me, He was a mentor—the ultimate Mentor. He taught truth and mentored those who would receive Him. Look at His time with the disciples. After performing miracles, He would go away to spend time with the Father and His followers. That must tell us something, right?

> # WE WERE CALLED TO DISCIPLE
> # AND TO BE DISCIPLED

Did you know that in Japan, the only professional who does not have to bow before the emperor is the teacher? Why do you think that is?

The Bible makes it clear that we were called to disciple and to be discipled. What does that mean? We were called to learn and to teach. We are all parts of the body of Christ. If you are called to be a hand, if that is your purpose—learn from a great hand, and become the best hand you can be. But don't let it stop there. Teach other hands how to be the best hands they can be so they can do the same for other hands. I believe that is the original design.

People Will Hurt Us, but We Must Love Them Anyway

The year 2016 was crazy for me, both positively and negatively. I started the year being one of seventeen entrepreneurs selected from among one thousand who applied to be personally mentored by a Brazilian billionaire for three days in Orlando in a program called Millionaire Legacy. And I ended the year being mentored by someone who has a beautiful international ministry that touches people's lives all over the world.

In between, I was having a mental and emotional breakdown. A complete identity crisis.

I was so far down in the pit, I couldn't even see the light anymore. I had no idea who I was or where I was going. But it didn't end there. Like Larry, I was also persecuted and publicly accused of something I never did. I always say that when you are doing something wrong, you expect that one day it will show up and you will pay the price, but you are at least prepared.

What happens when you are not?

What happens when you have done everything you possibly could to make sure things were done right, and all of a sudden, someone shows up and accuses you of something horrible? How can you be prepared for something like that?

These situations and experiences developed within me such a bitter feeling toward people that I decided to eliminate any type of relationship I had, to the point that I almost lost my family and myself in the process. What saved me was Larry telling me that even though he had gone through something similar, he would not allow that to hold him back from loving people. That is the best investment he could ever make. Always. No matter what people did and will always do to him, he has chosen to love people anyway.

After being with him for a few weeks, I finally concluded that we were all created for relationships. The moment you remove that from your life, everything starts crumbling. You slowly start dying, getting further away from your ultimate purpose in life.

Remember this: hurt people will always hurt people. Our job is to love people when they hate us. To feed them when they are hungry. To give them something to drink when they are thirsty. To clothe them when they are cold.

But I say, love your enemies! Pray for those who persecute you! (Matt. 5:44)

God is good. He rescued me. I just had to take the first step; He did the rest. That's how awesome He is. He is a good Father. He is the best mentor we will ever have.

Get to know Him. Develop a relationship with Him. You won't regret it. If you don't know how to get started, find someone who can help you through it. Maybe I can help you. You have taken the first step: you are reading this book. The seed is there. Allow your heart to be fertile ground, and remember that the more "fertilizer" people may throw at you, the more the seed will grow and eventually be turned into a strong tree that will bear much fruit.

The best investment you can ever make is in other people and in yourself. Don't be afraid to invest your time and resources in yourself and in your lifelong education, through books, courses, and mentorship programs. Put down the remote for the TV. Pick up that book that was written by the person you admire the most. Go hear that person speak. Spend time with good people who will speak life into you for a change. Give up a weekend here and there to learn, develop, and grow. Find your Larry. Become a Larry to someone else. It will be worth it. I guarantee it.

CHAPTER

08

Steps on The Journey of a Kingsman

Let's review the steps from this chapter that will lead you to your ultimate goal of becoming a Kingsman:

1. Nurture your relationships with others; they are vital to your well-being.

2. Find a mentor to help you grow.

3. Be a mentor to someone else, when you are ready.

4. Forgive those who have hurt you, even if—especially if—they don't deserve it. It isn't easy, but God expects us to forgive others if He is to forgive us. Forgiveness is the ultimate freedom.

QUEST SIX
FAMILY

CHAPTER 09

A Lasting Legacy

"Have you ever had an affair?" my wife, Daniela, asked.

I said, "Yes."

At first, Daniela didn't think I understood what she'd asked me. She asked again to be sure, almost laughing as she said, "I know I've asked you this many times, and I promise this is the last time I will ask you. Have you ever been unfaithful?"

Again, I said, "Yes."

Daniela vividly remembers the pain she felt at that moment:

Time sat still. I couldn't believe it. Diogo told me all about what had happened and told me whom it had happened with. "Are you serious?" I kept thinking. He told me the whole story. I couldn't hold the tears back. Sitting at this beautiful restaurant, five hundred feet up in the air at the top of Reunion Tower in Dallas, in this beautiful place he had picked for our anniversary, my life had begun to fall apart.

I couldn't stop crying. I couldn't believe it. So I left. But I had nowhere to go and no way to get anywhere. He had the keys for our only vehicle. And he had the valet ticket.

As I rode the elevator down to the lobby and walked toward the front of the hotel where the restaurant was located, trying to breathe, I could not stop crying. I was having a horrible nightmare, and I just wanted to wake up. I couldn't believe it.

Diogo had also come downstairs, so we got into the car. I yelled at him the whole thirty minutes on our ride home. Whenever he would try to say something, I would just tell him to shut up. I do not curse. But I couldn't stop cursing that day. I didn't know how to express my desperation. My whole marriage was a lie.

We got home, and I went straight to the bedroom. I still could not stop crying. The kids were asleep. He dismissed the babysitter and went to see Larry. I wasn't even able to tell him what was going through my mind at that time.

What kind of person would I be if I had left every time he had acted a particular way? When he was depressed, living with him was not easy. He was sick, so I couldn't leave. I stuck by him the whole time he was going through depression. But now I know what was going on during that time. That made me even madder. I had stood by his side the entire time.

His mother was the only one with me the whole time he was going through depression. That night when I got home, I called her and told her everything. She cried and prayed with me. For a few weeks, I could hardly speak to him. I couldn't function. He took care of the kids. I was numb.

It was all supposed to be just a beautiful time on our thirteenth anniversary. I wanted it to be a perfect day. It was at a wonderful place. Everything was going so well. We had such a beautiful connection that day. Or so I thought.

When I asked him that question, I was so sure the answer would be no. I could see how he had been seeking God and getting so close to Him and us at the same time. He had never been that close to us before. I wanted us to raise our kids to serve God and follow Jesus. I saw over the previous month how he had changed and become the person I had always wanted him to be. Now this was happening.

Face Your Dangerous Tendencies

Why am I including this story in this book? Why am I revealing my terrible choices to you? Because I need to be transparent here. After all, I did promise you this in the beginning. True community is a place of authenticity, not performance. And it is a place of healing and family. But to be personally healed and to lead a healthy family, I had to face my dangerous tendencies.

In the previous chapter, I highlighted the power of mentorship. Now I want to focus on family—on the ability to leave a true legacy behind. With that, I need you to be able to not only see it but to also understand that you will not be able to become the person you need to be unless you have mentors you can speak to, guides to lead you as they travel with you on this quest. That involves addressing the issues that stand in the way of you reaching your true potential.

If we claim we have no sin, we are only fooling ourselves and not living in the truth. But if we confess our sins to him, he is faithful and just to forgive us our sins and to cleanse us from all wickedness. If we claim we have not sinned, we are calling God a liar and showing that his word has no place in our hearts (1 John 1:8–10).

After my confession, Daniela and I both needed people we could talk to, people who would listen. I immediately called Larry and drove to his house. Larry's daughter, Trina, works with couples, so we contacted her the next day. Coincidence? I don't think so. God needed to take us all the way to Texas because He knew that for true healing to take place, we would need to be in the right environment, surrounded by people who would love us—no matter what.

We Must Forgive Each Other

The sessions with Trina were life-changing. She showed us the roots of the problems we were facing and how they had started many years before. Understanding it all helped us both. Daniela says, "I needed to work toward forgiveness." She continues:

The turning point was being willing to work toward forgiveness. I read a book, and we went through the counseling sessions. Trina told me, "You are going to choose if you will stay or leave, but I believe you will see he has changed."

Forgiveness was still very hard. Then I heard Pastor Robert Morris preach on forgiveness, saying Jesus died on the cross to forgive every sin. God forgives. We must forgive, no matter what was done to us.

It was a choice. We sat down after the service, and I told Diogo, "I forgive you." Though it still wasn't easy, it was right. My feelings didn't immediately change, but having Trina walk with me through this was healing.

"It's not going to be quick. But you will get there," she said.

My biggest reason to stay was to see the changes in his life. He was a different person. He was at a turning point. He was seeking God. I had not seen him live this way before. But yes, it was a process. A painful and long one at that.

Today I can proudly and surely say I can tell him anything. He can tell me anything. It is a real marriage. We walk through life together, instead of separately. I look back and see God's favor. It is almost unbelievable.

What suggestions would I give to others? The first thing I would say is that your relationship with God has to be a priority. There is no other way. It is only through Him that we can forgive others. If it wasn't for God's strength, I could not have forgiven Diogo. God can lift pain. Something was lifted from inside me when I was willing to forgive. No matter what has been done to you, forgiveness is the best thing that could ever happen to you. People say it is not fair. It is all about you. But the truth is that forgiveness is the best thing that could ever happen to you. You are not doing it for the other person but for yourself. People hold on to their grudges because they think the other person doesn't deserve their forgiveness. No matter what happens in life, we must forgive.

Having someone you trust walk you through this journey is crucial. It is not an easy one. You are trying to do something that goes against the natural response and what the enemy wants. It's completely counterintuitive from a natural perspective. Diogo didn't deserve to be forgiven! For months, things constantly came into my mind. "Stupid!" "Why?" "Just walk away."

Right before we moved to Texas, when he first walked away from everything we had built over the years, he told his dad, who was his business partner, that he was leaving but didn't want to take anything with him. I didn't quite understand what he was doing, and to be honest, I didn't really accept it well. But after going through this situation and seeing how, if I decided to leave, he would again be willing to leave literally everything behind and walk away empty-handed, I started to understand that a real change in his life had taken place. As I struggled through this painful process, I would often reach out and talk to Trina. She knew exactly how to help me. She had been there as well.

Find someone who knows the pain themselves. Sing songs, pray prayers, and seek counseling. Move back to God. Even though you may think you know the answer, sometimes the "voices" of discouragement, desperation, and frustration are louder. Ask Him for strength and wisdom to know how to deal with your emotions and thoughts. Again, make sure you have someone helping you get back on track.

If you forgive those who sin against you, your heavenly Father will forgive you. But if you refuse to forgive others, your Father will not forgive your sins (Matt. 6:14–15).

Release All Bitterness

I wish you could see how much of an impact this whole process has had on my entire family. How God used all these problems to bring us close together. This is a process, and a painful one at that, but if it doesn't start today and more importantly with you, when then? With whom?

Bitterness needs to be released. This might be a test—an opportunity to

> # WE HAVE TROUBLE LOVING OTHERS BECAUSE WE DON'T LOVE OURSELVES

get over the past pains. We have trouble loving others because we don't love ourselves.

Families are hurting. Love and acceptance are missing in families' lives nowadays.

If somebody in your family is being mean to you, you don't have to be mean back. They have issues. Refuse to let their issues become your issues. Treat them better. Refuse to respond by copying their behavior.

For husbands, this means love your wives, just as Christ loved the church. He gave up his life for her to make her holy and clean, washed by the cleansing of God's word. He did this to present her to himself as a glorious church without a spot or wrinkle or any other blemish. Instead, she will be holy and without fault. In the same way, husbands ought to love their wives as they love their own bodies. For a man who loves his wife actually shows love for himself (Eph. 5:25–28).

We Must Cherish Our Families

I honestly believe we should not be allowed to get married and have children unless we have been through an intensive program all our lives that will teach us how to actually do that.

My family is by far the most important thing to me in this world. My home is my heaven; I want to come back home every night. That wasn't always the case. On the last day of our lives, the only regret I believe we will have is that we didn't spend enough time with the ones we loved. I have put my family through a lot, and it hurts me just to think about it. I believe the goal of life is to leave a lasting legacy—a map others can follow. The generational curse needs to end with someone. For months, I asked God to end it with me, even if it cost my life.

I want to look at my family every day and realize what a privilege it is to get a chance to be there for them. Sometimes I just sit and watch them, and I can hardly believe how lucky I am. An overwhelming sense of gratitude comes over me. Tears come to my eyes.

Many people today have no idea what is it like to be a family. Everyone is doing their own thing, and the whole situation is completely dysfunctional. People often are amazed by how polite our kids act. Are we amazing parents? No, but we talk *to* them, not *at* them. We tell them how much we love them, how important they are, and that they are awesome and were uniquely created by an amazing God. We build them up daily the best way we can.

FAMILY IS THE FOUNDATION OF EVERYTHING

Family is the foundation of everything—there is no world without family. My wife is my rock. I would not be where I am today had she not been by my side. My admiration, love, and respect for her grow more each day. She becomes even more beautiful as the years go by.

How does she do it? How does someone go through what she went through all those years, and after hearing about every single detail of what I had done, come out on the other end victorious? I am not saying we haven't been full of wounds that are slowly being healed, but we are victorious nevertheless. I could say today, without a shadow of a doubt, that if I were given the option to choose between my life or hers, I would absolutely choose hers. I am not saying this just because it is the right thing to say. I really mean it.

God Turned My Mess into a Message

I have met with so many people over the years who, like me, went into their marriages wondering if things were going to work out and figuring that if they didn't, they would just call it quits. That is the level of uncertainty that my wife had to go through for so many years, and because I have always been very vocal about everything, I would make sure she understood it. How does someone put up with something like that? I know for a fact that I married up. Daniela is smart, caring, kind, good, faithful, patient, and beautiful. She could have anyone she wanted; why, then, did she decide to stick around? It never made sense in my head, other than it was God-appointed.

I never intentionally wanted to hurt her. I actually wanted to find a way to give her a way out without feeling guilty. After going through so much with me, that is the least I could do, right? I thought that if she were to find out what I had done, she would leave me and never feel guilty about it. It sounded like a good plan—or so I thought. Twisted, isn't it? Little did I know how God would use this whole mess for something greater.

Who knows? Maybe you are going through something like this right now. Maybe He used my *mess* and turned it into my *message* so you could read it right now. But I need to be honest with you. You can try to hide all you want, but you will never have the peace you are looking for until you face your demons head-on. How do I know? I tried to hide my sins for a very long time. The dark spots in your life need to be exposed for true healing to take place. As much as it hurts, it needs to happen, but this decision can only come from you. To leave a lasting legacy once you are gone requires that you live within God's will now.

CHAPTER
09

Steps on The Journey
of a Kingsman

Let's review the steps from this chapter that will lead you to your ultimate goal of becoming a Kingsman:

1. Face your dangerous tendencies—the ones that put your relationships with your loved ones and God at risk.

2. Release all bitterness, and replace it with love and forgiveness.

3. Cherish your family.

4. Turn your hardships into lessons learned, both for yourself and others.

QUEST SEVEN
WEALTH

CHAPTER 10

The Power of Passive Income

When my older son, Matthew, was only five years old, he said to me, "Daddy, I already know what kind of car I want to have when I grow up."

It amazed me. At such an early age, he already had something so clear on his mind, even if it was just the type of car he would want to have when he finally reached an age at which he could drive.

I said, "Really, Mattie? That's awesome!" Then I went on about my business, thinking he was only playing around.

"I want an Audi R-8, just like the one Iron Man has—but I want it in red," he continued.

I wish you could have been there to see the look on my face as I picked him up, put him in my lap, and asked him to tell me more about it. You can only imagine how excited I was to know that my five-year-old son not only had his first clear and specific goal in mind but had also picked something that most people would view as either a waste of money—because the car does cost about $120,000, after all—or as something completely impossible to achieve.

Dream Huge Dreams

Many people would suggest that I should have given my five-year-old son a lecture on not having such high goals and expectations because he could potentially develop a sense of frustration if he never achieved the goal. Others might say I should help him start a process of flat-out killing the incredible drive he already had. They would argue that I shouldn't encourage him to do something extraordinary with his life and to have an amazing opportunity to get great rewards along the way. They would want me instead to teach him to simply go to school, get good grades so he could then get into a good university that would empower him to get a good job, and spend the next forty years of his life doing something he would not be passionate about so that he could then hopefully retire by age sixty-seven and live on 40 percent of what he couldn't live on his entire life to begin with.

Does any of this sound familiar? What a great plan most people grow up with, don't you think?

So I did what most parents would never even dream of doing: I immediately Googled the car's model name and color. I had Matthew pick out which one looked exactly like the one he had in mind. After all, it wasn't up to me to tell him what he should want since it seemed like he was crystal clear on his outcome—even at five years of age. Once he picked out the car that matched his dream, we printed out a picture of it so he could post it on the wall next to his bed and look at it every single day until he reached his ultimate goal. And even though it would be years before he could even get his driver's license, I wanted to make sure he never once lost his focus.

The piece of paper with his brand-new Audi R-8 was still warm from the printer as I handed it to him. He held it in his little hands as an amazing smile and an incredible sense of excitement came over him. "I am going to have this car when I am older, Daddy," he said.

I was so proud. For years, he had been observing his mom and me work hard to give him the life he now had. He watched our every move. He listened to every conversation we had. Little did we know that his young mind was being shaped by our words and actions.

Know Where You Are and Where You Are Going

Our parents always provided for us in a major way, and we now had a chance to give him a life beyond anything we had ever imagined. As he was walking out of my office, I couldn't miss the opportunity to make sure that, even though he was really clear and excited about that new goal, he understood how much of a commitment it would take if he really wanted to achieve it. I took a few extra minutes and asked him if he knew how much that car cost. He told me he had no idea. We quickly looked it up and found out what his dream car would cost. Using his own handwriting at the top of the page and right above the picture, I had him write down *Audi R-8 = $120,000*. Directly below the image, I had him write down *My Dream Car and* sign his name: *Matthew Esteves.* That picture stayed in his room for the longest time, and he still talks about this car—especially when the local Ferrari dealership we sometimes visit has the Audi R-8 on display.

Now, you may be thinking, "OK, Diogo, he wanted a nice car. What's so amazing about that?"

You see, it's not about the car. It's about the clear and specific goal he had in mind. It's about knowing exactly *where you are, where you are going,* and *what you need to do to get there.* It's about being able to develop such an amazing and compelling future for you and your family that when life gets in the way and things get tough, you don't feel the urge to simply give up. Instead, you have an amazing drive to keep pushing forward.

My dad taught me that it's easy to manage things when everything is going well. The challenge is being able to stay the course when things get ugly. That's when you finally discover whether or not you have a strong enough *why* in place to empower you to move past the challenges you currently face.

Purpose Is the Foundation of the Kingsman Journey

If you haven't realized it by now, there is a main theme throughout this book that is touched in each one of the quests and plays a major role in the overall Kingsman journey. That theme is *purpose.*

The reason I bring this up is because I have been showing you that every one of us has been given unique abilities and talents that we are to develop throughout our lives so we can become the men and women we were created to be. It is up to us to discover how we can use our unique abilities to impact the lives of the people around us by becoming the part of the body we were called to be, benefiting the body as a whole.

Because of the privilege and authority God has given me, I give each of you this warning: Don't think you are better than you really are. Be honest in your evaluation of yourselves, measuring yourselves by the faith God has given us. Just as our bodies have many parts and each part has a special function, so it is with Christ's body. We are many parts of one body, and we all belong to each other. In his grace, God has given us different gifts for doing certain things well. So if God has given you the ability to prophesy, speak out with as much faith as God has given you. If your gift is serving others, serve them well. If you are a teacher, teach well (Rom. 12:3–7).

Because I have always enjoyed playing with numbers and have spent most of my adult life developing my skills in the financial services arena in the areas of insurance, mortgage, investments, and real estate, you can only imagine how much fun I am having writing these two chapters on the wealth quest. This is how I get to operate in my gifts and fulfill my God-given purpose in life.

Debt Isn't Bad After All

I am writing this now because, like most people, I grew up thinking that debt is bad. So naturally, when Matthew first came up to me and said he wanted a car, the first thought to enter my mind was that he is going

> I GREW UP THINKING THAT DEBT IS BAD

to have to work really hard for years to be able to put enough money together to be able to buy that car with cash—because I was brought up to believe that debt is always a bad choice.

Or, is it? I said that was my first thought because although I grew up with this limiting belief, after being in real estate for a few years now, I know that the best way—and in my opinion, the only way—to buy anything like a car, which is a depreciating liability—is to put little to no money down and to finance it for the rest of my life, if possible. I know this may seem completely counterintuitive, but I promise you, it will make complete sense when I tie it all together at the end of this quest.

Not too long ago, my wife and I had the opportunity to buy our dream cars. I had always wanted a Porsche Panamera, and she had always wanted a Range Rover Sport. After working hard for several years and having a few financial wins, we were finally able to treat ourselves to these amazing gifts. I wish you could have seen the look on her face as she opened the door to our house on that warm, sunny Florida morning and saw a beautiful white, customized Range Rover Sport sitting in our driveway. It was an amazing surprise.

That was on a Tuesday. On Thursday came another surprise. On our tenth wedding anniversary, I took her to Fort Lauderdale for the weekend to celebrate, and I prepared ten very special surprises to celebrate this important date: a beautiful designer hotel right on the beach, a stunning candlelight dinner, a boat ride, a gorgeous flower bouquet and an astonishing new three- carat diamond ring, among other things. The first surprise, though, was when I pulled up in my driveway to pick her up in a dazzling white Porsche Panamera. The look on her face was priceless. She asked me in awe, "What did you do?"

I thought about it for a second, wondering whether I should play along and come up with an incredible story, only to disappoint her in the end. I chose instead to just go with the hard, cold reality that I did not own the car. I told her it was only a rental for the weekend, but very soon we would be able to afford one.

That day finally came about one year later—almost to the day. And on the Thursday of the same week I had surprised her with her new car, I pulled up in my new pride and joy—an astonishing white Porsche Panamera, just like the one I had rented. You can only imagine how excited we were. Although these were only cars, they represented something bigger: our finances had finally taken a major positive turn after years of hard work.

Those two beauties had cost us a whopping $150,000, and guess what? I paid for them both with cash.

I hope that by now, you know that I am not trying to impress you with any of this. I want to guide you instead—guide you through an important lesson. I believe everything in my life has happened for a reason and couldn't have happened any other way. My life events have given me the opportunity to share these lessons and experiences with you today. And although I couldn't see this as we were going through the fire we have gone through, I am extremely thankful today that God was there to guide us every step of the way.

I often tell people when I share my story that if we had planned these past couple of years, they wouldn't have worked out as well as they did. But God planned it all before the foundation of the world, and for that I am forever grateful.

I Realized Years Later My Huge Mistake

Why am I telling you all of this? To brag about our achievements? Absolutely not! I am sharing my story to hopefully get you to understand that this was one of the biggest financial mistakes we have ever made. Buying the cars? No. Spending $150,000? Not at all. The biggest mistake we made was buying the cars with cash.

I know what you are probably thinking. I am perhaps out of my mind for even thinking I should have bought these cars with little to no money down and financed them for the rest of my life. I don't blame you one bit for thinking that way. That's how I thought for a long time. But I am here to tell you, that is exactly what I should have done. If you understand this one lesson, it will change your financial life forever.

But for that to happen, you need to go back and read Romans 12:2 again. This is definitely a huge part of changing the way you think. Do you know what I believe our biggest problem is? We are usually thinking just like everyone else around us.

It wasn't until I started surrounding myself with people who think differently from most people—and in turn achieve amazing results in life—that my life took a major turn for the better. I was finally able to break the chains that had kept me bound for so long.

Invest in Income-Producing Properties to Secure Your Future

Yes, I understand financing that much money would end up costing me a fortune every month—$2,500, to be exact. And to spend that much money on a car payment every month is completely ridiculous, right? Or is it?

What if I told you that I could have taken that same amount of money and bought five income-producing properties instead and had "passive income"—money rolling in without laboring at a desk job or manual job? What if I told you that I could still be driving the same exact cars, but because my properties were bought right, and the numbers made sense, I wouldn't have to work a single hour of the day to make my monthly car payments? Better yet, what if I told you that I could own the five properties and the two cars and still have $1,000 left over at the end of every month in my pocket—month in and month out—to do with as I please? Would you be interested in knowing how in the world that could possibly happen?

Boy, do I wish I could go back in time and hand my seventeen-year-old self the formula I am about to share with you. It would have completely changed my entire life around. Don't get me wrong; I am thankful for the life I have had so far. But after putting all the numbers from the past thirteen years down on paper, I realized how many poor choices I made just to try to fulfill a sense of instant gratification that never seems to be satisfied.

Yet true godliness with contentment is itself great wealth (1 Tim. 6:6).

If I had been equipped with the right information, emotional intelligence, mentorship and accountability, I would have, without a doubt, chosen a path that would lead me to ultimate financial freedom a lot sooner in life. Let's just say I am extremely excited to not only be able to apply this strategy in my life today but also get to share it with you, and more importantly, pass it on to my sons and see my entire family tree changing from now on, leaving a true legacy behind.

Let's just say I wish I could have had the last fruit of the spirit—self-control—in action back then. But again, the experience that would completely revolutionize my life and allow me to have the fruits of the Spirit operating within me wouldn't come into play until about two years later, with my final surrender.

In the next chapter, I am going to show you exactly what I could have done to change this situation around. I know it will blow your mind because it will allow you to look at your financial game through a completely different lens and, in turn, be able to change your entire family's future.

CHAPTER

10

Steps on The Journey
of a Kingsman

Let's review the steps from this chapter that will lead you to your ultimate goal of becoming a Kingsman:

1. Dream huge dreams.

2. Know where you are and where you are going.

3. Know your God-given purpose; it is the foundation of the Kingsman Journey.

4. Strengthen your financial future by investing in income-producing real estate.

5. Understand how to use debt wisely to free up your cash for revenue-producing investments.

6. Be a good steward of your money to honor God and your family.

Begin with the End in Mind

Before we start this chapter, I must warn you: unless you are a numbers person, you might have a bit of a challenge keeping up. I could be wrong, of course. But I have found out over the years that we are all different, which is the beauty behind it all. Maybe you can see and understand things that I would never be able to see and understand. In case you haven't realized by now, I really have a thing for numbers. I simply love them. So it's hard to stop me when I start talking about this. It might seem like drinking from a fire hose. But I promise that if you stick with me until the end, it will all make a lot of sense.

Have Investments and Money Left Over

I am going to make this as simple as possible so you can have a good idea of what I am talking about. I want you to be able to walk away with something you can apply in your life today—and use to achieve amazing

> KNOW WHAT YOUR FINANCIAL AND LIFE GOALS ARE FIRST, AND THEN WORK TO ACHIEVE THEM

results. When it comes to your financial future, you must plan now to reach a goal. You must begin with the end in mind. Know what your financial and life goals are first, and then work to achieve them. Pretty obvious, right?

As I mentioned in the previous chapter, debt is not a problem. Even bad debt isn't a problem. Eating cake is not a problem. The challenge is knowing how much, when to eat it, and what type of cake to eat so you don't end up putting on unwanted weight. The debtor is only a slave to the lender when he must be the one who has to go to work every day to pay for his debt.

Think about it. If someone else is paying your debt for you, then are you really a slave to the lender? For years, I have seen this being taught in churches and Christian financial programs all around the world. It frustrates me at a level you can't even begin to comprehend. The only thing I can think of is that most people simply don't understand how money really works.

As in my earlier example, with $150,000 in hand, I could have gone out and found five properties that were each worth around $120,000. Given time, I could have found a few property owners who, because of unwanted circumstances, would be more than willing to sell me their properties at a discount—say $20,000 less than they were worth. With that, I could have bought the properties for $100,000 each and immediately have an unrealized initial equity gain of about $100,000 among all five properties.

You might be thinking, "OK, Diogo, but that doesn't make any sense because you had only $150,000 in hand, not $500,000." You are absolutely right. That is why I mentioned earlier that unless you are willing to change the way you think, you will have a very hard time getting anywhere in life because in this situation, I would have to be willing to eliminate the limiting belief most of us have—that debt is bad. Why? Because for this to work, I would need to acquire five mortgages at $80,000 each, which would allow me to put 20 percent down on each property, or $100,000 as the total down payment on this deal. I would then use the additional $50,000 I would have left over from the initial amount for closing costs, reserves, and some potential initial remodeling of those properties. I would then get the properties ready to rent. Here's what the numbers should ideally look like:

- Gross rent (normally about 1 percent per month of the property value if you buy it right): $1,200/month

- PITI (principal and interest payments plus insurance and property taxes): $500/month
- Net rent: $700/month

Now, take the $700 for each property every month and add it all up. That's $3,500 coming in every month, after expenses. It's money in your pocket, month in and month out. Would I have to buy the cars? Of course not! But again, had I chosen to still buy them, this amount would have allowed me to make my $2,500 car payment and still have $1,000 left to do as I please every single month. And the most important part: I could do it without trading my time for dollars. I will talk more about this when we cover the time quest. I hope you were able to grasp this transformational truth—it's the same $150,000!

Why did I tell you all of this? Because you need to understand one thing. When it comes to your financial life, your focus should be *to do anything and everything you can to acquire as many income-producing assets as you possibly can so they can generate enough passive income to meet and exceed your monthly expenses.* That way, you can wake up each morning and decide whether or not you want to go work that day or simply take the day off and go have fun with your family.

Develop a Strong Real Estate Portfolio

Can you imagine living a life like this? Impossible, you may say. And if you believe it in your mind with all your strength and all your heart that living life this way is impossible, you are absolutely right. After all, as a man thinks, so he is.

I plead with you, especially if you are just starting on this journey: stop buying things you don't need with money you don't have to impress people who don't even like you. It is flat-out silly. Focus on developing a strong real estate portfolio or any other type of income-producing asset that allows you to have income today—not thirty years from now—so you can free up your time as fast as possible, pursue your God-given calling and fulfill your purpose on this Earth without having to ever worry or even think about money again. This truth will set you free and allow you to live a life of total abundance and complete financial freedom while helping you meet other people's needs. I promise you.

> *As you know, you Philippians were the only ones who gave me financial help when I first brought you the Good News and then traveled on from Macedonia. No other church did this (Phil. 4:15).*

Matthew will still have his Audi R-8, no doubt about it. But he now knows that he will buy it only when he has enough passive income to be able to cover his monthly payments. He knows he is not going to pay cash for it. He knows he is going to put little to no money down. He knows he is going to get a loan for as long as he possibly can because as long as he has that passive income coming in every month, the car payments will never be a problem because he will not have to go to work to ever make those payments. He knows he is not a slave to the lender—for either properties or a car—because his tenants are the ones who are funding his lifestyle. So, to improve his life, the only thing he will need to do is acquire more income-producing assets that will, in turn, generate even more passive income.

It's simple math. You must understand the rules of the game before you start playing it. I hope you realize by now how important this is.

To put this into perspective, I want to share with you that had I known what I know today, I could have retired by age thirty with a $7,000-per-month passive income for the rest of my life. If I had just learned this one simple principle when I first started my financial journey at seventeen years old, my life would be completely different today. That's how powerful this strategy is.

Matthew already has more than $2,000 saved as I am writing this book. Not because we just gave him a bunch of money, but because he has been saving up his monthly allowance, cash gifts he receives from others, proceeds from artwork he creates and sells to family and friends, and the occasional massage he offers everyone and charges anywhere from $1 to $5. Matthew has a very clear goal in mind. He has also learned from my mistakes. I hope you will, too.

Be Clear about What You Want in Life

Now, because we are talking about starting with the end in mind, I have just shared with you an amazing technique that has cost me hundreds of thousands of dollars and an incredible amount of time to learn. I want to share with you how to use it to your advantage. Most people do not have an *income* problem; they have a *clarity* problem. They don't know what they want, so no matter how much money they make, they will always end up in the same situation they were in to begin with. Ever wonder why most people who win the lottery or inherit a lot of money end up broke after just three short years?

Let's be real here for a second. There are only three reasons why most people are not growing financially. I mean, most of them believe that this is all rocket science. But it isn't. The problem is that they have:

- No idea where they *are*
- No idea where they are *going*
- No idea *how* to get there

I know this might be a little scary if you've never done this before. But if I were able to show you exactly how to do it and guide you the entire way, would you be open to learning? The thing is that we get in life exactly what we are willing to put into it. If you are willing to learn, I am willing to teach. And I am not just thinking about you; I am thinking about your family. I am thinking about how this whole thing is going to impact their lives for the better.

Yes, you are going to see amazing results in your own life. But imagine being able to see your kids grow up with this sort of knowledge. Imagine this being second nature to them. What would your life look like today if your parents had done this for you? And imagine being able to pass down this sort of wisdom to the people you love and care about the most. How much of an impact would this type of wisdom have in their lives?

The truth is that creating a compelling future isn't rocket science. But unless you have a formula, it becomes nearly impossible. Whether you like it or not, having clarity about where you want to be three, seven, and even twenty-one years from now is essential to your success. Understanding exactly where you are going will impact the daily decisions you make about money, regardless of what you do for a living or even how much money you make monthly.

Know Your Current Financial Position

Once you are clear on where you are going, you will need to understand where you are. And I say this because, although most people think they know exactly where they are, they really have no idea. Most of them have never had anyone who could show them their current financial position. All they know is that they are working to pay bills but have no clue about where they really stand.

Imagine being able to save your marriage because you now have such amazing clarity. Imagine being able to educate your kids properly so they never get into the bad financial situations you have been through your entire life. Imagine being able to live the life you want because everything simply works. How incredible would that be?

Once you know where you are going, as well as where you are, then you can learn how to get there in the most efficient way. And the way to go from A to Z is to have an effective strategy that will allow you to get there in the shortest period of time. It's important to understand that your financial strategy needs to be specific to your unique needs and situation to be sustainable. Constantly trying to keep up with the Joneses will take you down a path of frustration and ultimate failure. Trust me, I have been down that road, and that is the last place you would ever want to be.

Let me ask you a question: When was the last time you took a good class on how to build an effective strategy for your financial future? If you are like most people, you have taken history, science, and a lot of other classes you have never used your entire life, haven't you? However, the one thing you use every single day, you have never taken a class on. Coincidence? No wonder most people can't get it right. It's not your fault. The system has failed you. The system was built to make you fail. It was built in a way that for a few to win, many have to lose.

Fair? Not at all. But what is fair in life? You need to do your part because if you don't, no one will do it for you. Your family depends on you. Do it for them. I know you can. Just believe it and take action.

Keep More of What You Earn

To prove you can, let me tell you about a guy named Theodore Johnson. He was a UPS worker who, although never having made more than $14,000 per year, died with a net worth of $70 million. Now, how in the world did he do that? Here's the thing: you don't have a money problem; you have a strategy problem. It's never about how much you make. It's always about how much you keep and, more importantly, what you do with it to make it grow. What does that tell you? It tells me that hard work and luck are not enough if you want to create and sustain wealth. You must learn the rules of the game, period.

As you can see, there are a few key elements that must come into play if you ever want to reach a place in your financial life where your family is completely taken care of, no matter what. Yes, you can make a ton of money, but at the end of the day, unless you know how to manage and protect it properly, you will end up losing track of it and likely find yourself in a huge mess.

When it comes to your finances, you can spend your entire life building an empire, but if you don't learn how to properly protect it with the right type of coverage and specific instructions that will dictate exactly what should happen to your kids and possessions, even if you were no longer here, the first storm that comes around will cause everything to come crumbling down.

Use Leverage to Optimize Your Investments

It is also important to understand that leverage (using other people's money, time, and knowledge) will be your best friend when it comes to

> LEVERAGE (USING OTHER PEOPLE'S MONEY, TIME, AND KNOWLEDGE) WILL BE YOUR BEST FRIEND

growing your money and maximizing your overall returns by building and maintaining your credit score the right way. If you understand this concept, you will be able to use leverage to your full advantage and, in turn, completely optimize the way you invest.

The biggest problem, as I mentioned earlier, is not that you don't make enough throughout your lifetime; the problem is that you have no idea what to do with it. It's not just about growing it. It's also about understanding the rules first so you know exactly where to put your hard-earned money.

I know this might all sound very new to you and even a bit overwhelming, but I want to be the first one to tell you that you have nothing to worry about and, in the end, it will all make sense. All I need you to understand at this point is that unless you first learn how to change the way you think about your finances and how you relate to money, the tools you use will make no difference. You will always default to your old ways and always get the same bad results.

Knowledge is power, yes, but only when you apply it. Allow this truth to sink in and make a difference in your life and the lives of the people around you. Begin now to change the way you think and relate to money, and start building a secure financial future for your family. Begin with the end in mind. And keep this thought always in the forefront of your mind: no one builds an effective strategy to fail; they simply fail to build an effective strategy to achieve success in life.

CHAPTER

11

Steps on The Journey of a Kingsman

Let's review the steps from this chapter that will lead you to your ultimate goal of becoming a Kingsman:

1. Begin with the end in mind. Know what your financial and life goals are first, and then work to achieve them.

2. Be clear about what you want in life.

3. Know your current financial position.

4. Keep more of what you earn.

5. Use leverage to optimize your financial well-being.

QUEST EIGHT

CONTRIBUTION

CHAPTER 12

The Power of Forgiveness

The year 2017 was the toughest year of my life. I don't say this lightly or from a victim perspective or mentality. And it wasn't just my personal life; every aspect of my life was difficult.

I have always been a very driven individual, at least as far back as I can remember. So when I look back at everything that happened in 2017, it is a true a miracle that I was able to get through it.

God Wants Us to Be Still and Listen for His Voice

Ever since I met Larry, he has been telling me one thing: "You need to learn to relax." He would often tell me, "You have never relaxed your entire life." Wasn't that the truth? Being able to just sit still and listen for a split second has probably always been the most difficult task for me. Not because someone had added yet another label to my life such as ADHD, but because, for some reason, I felt a constant sense that I always

> # I FELT A CONSTANT SENSE THAT I ALWAYS NEEDED TO BE SHOWING RESULTS

needed to be showing results, at all times, no matter what.

If I was at the beach, I had to be on my phone to make sure I didn't miss a single call from a potential client. If I was at a party, I needed to make sure I was prospecting and collecting information. I believe a lot of that came from the first company I worked for as a self-employed individual, where I was 100 percent on commission. They taught us that we should always be prospecting and that no matter what the circumstances were, there was always an opportunity to do business. The challenge with that was that over the years, I was never able to simply relax, let alone enjoy what I had built. Just to put into perspective, in a one-year period, my wife and I won two all-expenses-paid trips to San Diego and Hawaii.

Did I enjoy those experiences? Not one bit. Why? That's the worst part—I had no idea. Not only that, but it got to a point where the only thing I could talk about all the time, no matter where I was or who I was with, was doing business. As you can imagine, that didn't get the people around me to say, "Hey, let's hang out." I figured that if I couldn't stand myself, others couldn't, either. That was a true prison. I believe God wants us to be still and listen for His guidance. We can't do that when we are consumed with the details of the world around us.

The Amazing Resilience of a Child

In case you haven't noticed, I am extremely passionate about my kids, and I love both of them equally. Lucca, who is only three years old, is an amazing child who has a personality like no other. I love the fact that he just looks at us sometimes, with that cute little smile of his, puts my and my wife's hands together, holds them tightly, and says: "I love you so much, you guys." That really makes my heart smile. He is the kind of kid who lifts you up, no matter how down you might be that day, by using simple words and gestures. It is truly amazing. We are blessed beyond words.

Matthew, on the other hand, who is only nine years old, has been through more than most people go through in an entire lifetime. I believe that he is, without a doubt, the biggest inspiration I have in life at this point.

Then God said, "Let us make human beings in our image, to be like us. They will reign over the fish in the sea, the birds in the sky, the livestock, all the wild animals on the earth, and the small animals that scurry along the ground." So God created human beings in his own image. In the image of God he created them; male and female he created them. Then God blessed them and said, "Be fruitful and multiply. Fill the earth and govern it. Reign over the fish in the sea, the birds in the sky, and all the animals that scurry along the ground." (Gen. 1:26–28).

Let me explain Matthew's situation so it makes sense. As I mentioned in an earlier chapter, he was born at twenty-nine weeks, spent two months in the NICU, and has been through eight surgeries. As if that wasn't enough, at birth, he was diagnosed with cerebral palsy. Yet he is such an amazing and smart kid. I don't say this lightly or just because I am his father. Everyone who meets him says the same thing. I hope you can meet him one day. He is a true champion. Resilience is something that, thank God, Matthew, Daniela, and I have been blessed with, and I am sure Lucca will be, too.

Daniela was recently driving back home after picking up the kids from school. Matthew said he wanted to tell her something. She noticed that he was a little uncomfortable, but being such an amazing kid, he was not going to allow that to hold him back.

He said, "Mommy, I want to tell you something," He continued, "I never told anyone this, but I was bullied for two years, between my schools in Orlando and Texas."

Tears started rolling down Daniela's face. "What do you mean?" she asked. "How come you never told us anything?"

As Daniela started to pull herself together to be able to offer him the comfort she thought he needed at that time, Matthew again amazed her with his words: "But don't worry, Mommy. The reason I am telling you this now is because, even though I know that what they did was wrong, I have already forgiven them. I have also already prayed for them because I understand now that if they hurt me, it was probably because they were hurting as well. Maybe they don't have good parents like I do or a good home to come back to every day. So really, don't worry."

You can only imagine what that did to my wife. To see our nine-year-old son do what most grown-ups would never even dream of doing, with such a kind heart and mature understanding, was an amazing experience and lesson to say the least. She quickly pulled up to our home and held him as tightly as she could, trying to get whatever pain was still there completely out of him.

Like any mother, she first felt rage. But after that incredible demonstration of compassion from a nine-year-old kid, what was she supposed to do? She loved on him and remembered what she had done months before when, at the top of Reunion Tower, I told her what I had done. She remembered how she was able to forgive me for what I did—because Jesus first forgave her.

When she told me that story, I couldn't hold my tears back. I have never been an emotional guy. I was taught that men don't show their emotions; it makes us look weak. But in the last couple of years, I have cried like a baby in every situation you can imagine. Sad and even happy moments. Movies and celebrations. Sometimes tears come rolling down my face just because I look at my family and realize how lucky I am. And I am proud to say that. I believe this is the way life should be. We shouldn't hold back something so beautiful that God has given us—the ability to demonstrate how we feel on the inside.

Work Can Consume Us

The reason I am telling you this is because, little did I know how much of an impact that one moment Daniela had in the car with Matthew was going to play in my own life. I mentioned earlier that 2017 was the hardest year I have ever had to endure in my life. But it didn't start that year. Looking back, I am thankful it happened because the way God used everything to completely change my life was incredible. My world was turned upside down, but it would eventually result in significant healing of tremendous pain—not only for myself, but for my entire family.

As I shared with you in an earlier chapter, after reaching the peak of what I thought success was, I had an emotional and mental meltdown, followed by an identity crisis caused by a series of events that had happened the previous year. I got to a place where I could barely think straight, let alone do the things any man would want to do to take care of his family.

All my life, I had been given labels such as "depressed," "bipolar," "greedy," and "arrogant." I never had, however, been called a thief. We often go through life focusing on ourselves, doing everything we can to grow in life and to provide for our families the best way possible. Sometimes we end up treating others in a way that we would never like to be treated. We do things we shouldn't do so we can get to a place we believe is going to give us what we are looking for. We say things we shouldn't say and even handle things in a way that someone who follows Christ never should.

Nevertheless, we are always trying to do everything we can the best way possible, following the rules and being able to lay our heads on our pillows at night and have a good night of sleep. This can happen only when we know that we have a clear conscience about the work we do on a daily basis that provides so many people the opportunity to turn their dreams into reality. So what happens when, because of a few individuals, that beautiful dream you have been working on for so long and have put so much love and effort into turns into a nightmare?

Up until 2014, I had never experienced what it was like to build a successful company, at least not personally. My father purchased a business, back in Brazil, about twenty years ago for $10,000, and now it is worth $1.5 million. So, even though I had a good sense of what I should do, I never really had any hands-on experience. What I knew is what I had seen my father and mother do all those years: work hard until it pays off. The more you work, the more you grow.

The challenge with that approach is that if you are not careful, work ends up consuming you. All of a sudden, there are no more family nights or weekends. Business is booming, yes, but the quality of your life is slowly imploding. Growing up, all I knew was how to trade time for money. The more time I gave, the more money I made. But here is where the problem lies: we have only twenty-four hours in a day, and we must balance them among work, family, and self-growth. What do you do then when the only solution you can find to the problem is to leverage other people's time, money, and resources? You suddenly have an epiphany.

My Idea Multiplies My Wealth

I finally realized that yes, I could keep trading my time for money and impact only one person at a time, or I could find a way to get my message out and help as many people as I possibly could. And that's exactly what I did. What I didn't know was that a little more than twelve months after I had that idea, the very thing that would cause me to start feeling even a small sense of contribution to the world would be the main thing that would haunt me for the next twelve months.

In 2012, I decided to get into real estate. Although I was doing fairly well working with insurance up until that moment, it seemed like I was trading all my time for money. The math just didn't add up. Let's say you had a choice between two scenarios. You could either work eighty hours a week, talk to hundreds of people to be able to write a few policies, and then bring home $10,000, or you could help one family turn their dream of having a small property in Mickey Mouse's backyard and make $12,000 instead, in about six hours, from beginning to end. Which would you choose? Not a tough call, right?

What happens then, when you suddenly start helping other families accomplish the same dream, but with a bigger home and you are now making $80,000 in the same six hours? You get hooked. That's what happens.

You suddenly realize that you are doing pretty well, and if you could only do ten of those per year, you would have a pretty decent lifestyle. You then start focusing all your time on what gives you the most—not just money, but a sense of significance, which is one of the basic human needs. You then decide that you no longer want to trade your time for money, so you take it a step further and start building a company and hiring other people to sell houses for you. You don't make the big bucks for each transaction anymore, but you now have twenty-five people out there who are helping other families turn their dreams of homeownership into reality, and you make a few thousand dollars from each of them to train and develop them daily.

Life becomes great. Or so you think, right? Because business is so good, you have people who have watched your growth but didn't quite believe in what you were doing in the beginning, now wanting to be your partners. After all, can you blame them? You had no experience in the beginning. Who could have possibly imagined this whole thing would work?

But then you have an idea. And although you don't want to bring partners into your main business, why not franchise the entire operation and not only get paid on what your agents are doing, but also be paid a percentage of what the franchisees do? Sounds like a good plan, right? Isn't it all about growing and being able to impact more and more people, without having to keep trading your time for money and finally being able to leverage other people's time, money, and knowledge?

You may be looking at this whole situation and either think I was crazy or, like most people, think this was anyone's dream come true. After all, this twenty-nine-year-old "boy" was living the dream life. I had a beautiful family, a beautiful home, incredible cars, and a successful company that in the first year in business had done $35 million in sales. That was more than twice what one of my competitors, who had been in business for twenty years, had that same year. And coincidentally, that had been the competitor's best year ever, at $16 million. What else could anyone ask for in life?

I will tell you: the ability to be able to feel like I was really giving back and to fulfill one of the needs of the spirit—contribution—and not simply grow exponentially with no purpose.

Just as the body is dead without breath, so also faith is dead without good works (James 2:26).

Success without Fulfillment Is the Ultimate Failure

The math simply just didn't add up in the end. After an explosively incredible year in business and in my personal finances, I felt miserable. It seemed like the more I grew, the bigger the void inside my heart became. I couldn't understand it. It didn't make any sense at all. Everyone around me would to try to figure out why I was so miserable. "Look at your life," they would say. "You have everything anyone would ever want." "Why can't you just be happy and enjoy it?" they constantly asked.

That was the million-dollar question, wasn't it? Why couldn't I? Why was it so difficult for me to simply stop along the way and smell the roses?

What happens when money and things stop making sense? What do you do when everything becomes colorless and tasteless and you completely lose the drive to do anything productive with your life? What I am about to share with you in the next couple of chapters will help you understand why we do what we do and the power that lies behind our ability to simply comprehend life when everything stops making sense.

CHAPTER

12

Steps on The Journey
of a Kingsman

Let's review the steps from this chapter that will lead you to your ultimate goal of becoming a Kingsman:

1. Be still, and listen for God's voice.

2. Strive for balance in your life; don't let work consume you.

3. Seek to fulfill your purpose, not just to make money. Success without fulfillment is the ultimate failure.

CHAPTER 13

The Power of Actions

When I first moved to the United States on my own, I was only seventeen years old. I was making $5 an hour plus tips, working as a busboy in a resort in Sun Valley, Idaho. Little did I know what would happen thirteen years later, when I finally decided to share with my fellow Brazilians what life in the United States had been like for me all those years. That was the beginning of what I thought my contribution to the world was.

As I mentioned before, a couple of years ago, I started a YouTube channel called "Um Brasileiro Na América," where I would share not only my story, but also my day-to-day interactions with people from Brazil who had a dream of moving to this incredible country one day. My wife and I opened the doors to our home. We shared personal stories, family trips, and even the best moments with our kids. People simply loved watching our channel, and, as I am writing this book, our videos have been seen more than two million times.

I just love thinking about how many lives we have touched through this one little project we started. We received messages almost daily from people thanking us for doing it and telling us how much of an impact we had caused. Who would have ever thought that something so simple would make such a difference in someone's life? I don't know about you, but I am all about impact, so this sort of thing really fires me up. This went on for a little less than a year, until something very unfortunate happened.

An Idea that Seemed Wise at the Time

When I was fourteen years old, my parents decided to leave Brazil behind and pursue the American Dream. They wanted to give us a better life. We moved to Fort Lauderdale so my father could help a church that was in the process of being established. It wasn't an easy process. My parents went from successful entrepreneurs in Brazil to cleaning offices and restaurants in Miami every day until 2:00 a.m. And although we didn't quite understand what was going on, we knew they were sacrificing their lives so we could have a better life.

Does that sound familiar? That's what any father and mother in their right mind would do, right? Over the years I have seen many people move to this country with big hopes and dreams, only to see it all fall apart after a few short months because of bad decisions, lack of information, and being taken advantage of. When you see something like that, you feel hopeless because you don't know what to do. In my search for meaning and to fill my big void, the YouTube channel was born. I mean, I couldn't change the world. But if I could share a little bit of joy and our experiences with others, as well as our personal story, then maybe, just maybe, I could start feeling alive again. And it worked, even if for a short time.

As I told you before, happiness comes from the inside. If you are trying to fill it with external things, it will work only for a little while, and you will then find yourself seeking the next high. After months of creating videos for the YouTube channel, we started getting a lot of requests to put something together where people could learn, in an organized and structured way, how they, too, could make the type of transition we had made.

Being not only a numbers person but also a business guy, I went to work immediately. I created a beautiful program that showed the step-by-step process that someone would need to do to make the transition smoothly. They wouldn't have to go through everything we had to go through to get to where we were. It didn't mean it was going to be easy. But the way I see it is, even though a *good* way to learn is from your own mistakes, a *great* way to learn is from other people's mistakes. This would at least give people an opportunity to learn from my mistakes.

So let's not get tired of doing what is good. At just the right time we will reap a harvest of blessing if we don't give up (Gal. 6:9).

At that point, I had already built quite a bit of a following—around 150,000 people on social media. And when I launched the free class that would eventually lead to the paid program, I had about 3,000 watching. But because it was a test program, I needed to hand-pick the people who would be participating with us. So, after going through a long and selective process, I ended up picking thirteen of the almost five hundred families who applied. The program was a success. We were able to get some great testimonials and build amazing relationships.

We Didn't See Devastation Coming

Again, I got a new external high that wouldn't last very long. While we were putting this program together, a family from Brazil contacted us and said they would like to hire us to help with their transition. We talked about the options, as well as the program we were putting together, but they were looking for a hands-on type of consultation.

They had watched a video on which another YouTube channel had interviewed me, where I explained how we could help not only get you in touch with the right professionals and guide you through the entire transition, but also help you and your family feel at home from the moment you set foot in this country. You would have your home completely ready, from furniture and decor all the way to bedding, pots, and pans, as well as a car, clean and gassed up in your garage, ready to go, and your kids registered in school, among other things. It was basically the life I would have loved to give my family if we had just moved to another country.

Yes, there was obviously a cost involved, but the peace of mind would have been completely worth it. So, after many conversations, this family decided to hire us to do exactly that. The process was great. Everyone was involved and excited. We exchanged multiple messages throughout the day, giving them not only what they had hired us to do, but also the emotional support we would have loved to have had when we first moved, because we know how stressful moving to a completely different country can be.

It was a dream come true. We had such a sense of contribution and fulfillment that we could hardly wait to finally be able to pick up this family at the airport and take them to their new life.

Then, halfway through the process, when most of the things we had been hired to do were already done, we got a message from them saying they wanted to cancel everything and for us to refund all their money. They said they had just found out that we had been taking advantage of

> # THEY WANTED TO CANCEL EVERYTHING AND FOR US TO REFUND ALL THEIR MONEY

people and stealing their money all over town and could not be trusted anymore. It's hard for me to share every single little detail here because this book would be twice as long. My goal is to drive a very specific lesson home when we tie it all together in the end.

By now, you are probably wondering if it was —had we been taking advantage of people and stealing their money? I was thirty-one at the time and doing extremely well financially but was as miserable as I could probably be. Why had I decided to start this entire project in the first place? Not because I needed more money, but because I badly needed to feel like I was giving back. And, yes, although this was a business transaction in the end and we had an entire team working on this project, money was the last motivation. With that, I am going to allow you to answer that question yourself.

*One of them, an expert in religious law, tried to trap him with this question: "Teacher, which is the most important commandment in the law of Moses?" Jesus replied, "You must love the L*ORD *your God with all your heart, all your soul, and all your mind.' This is the first and greatest commandment. A second is equally important: 'Love your neighbor as yourself.' The entire law and all the demands of the prophets are based on these two commandments"* (Matt. 22:35–40).

Others Can Resent Your Success

The problem if you haven't experienced that in your own life is that, when you start growing, most of the people around you start getting uncomfortable because they don't want you to change. It's understandable, after all. If you grow and they don't, will you stay? Of course not. Albert Einstein said that once a mind expands, it can never go back to what it used to be.

Have you even seen what happens when you put a few crabs inside a hole? The ones that are trying to get out will always be pulled back by the other ones who don't want to get out. It's comfortable where they are. Why do I bring this up? My growth in this city has, without a doubt, bothered a lot of people in our community.

I mean, how would you feel if you had been in business for years, never really seeing any true growth, and then all of a sudden, this twenty-eight-year-old "kid" comes into the game, builds a successful business that ends up attracting some of your agents and clients into his business, has explosive growth, and not only franchises it after just the first year and opens fifteen locations in the next year, but also develops an online following that takes most people ten years to build, in less than twelve months?

Please, I beg you to understand once again—none of this is meant to impress you. You need to understand that when you hit this sweet spot and understand the power that contribution has, you will have exponential growth in your life. With that, a lot of people are going to be bothered by it. They will do anything they can to destroy you and your reputation. They are looking for significance. They are not worrying about putting up a bigger building than yours. It's easier to just take yours down. To pull you back into the hole.

The sad thing is that this all came through the person who was helping them with their visa, so that person was technically a "reliable" source, right? This was someone I had referred them to. It wasn't a friend or even an acquaintance, but a professional who was highly recommended. She started this whole mess. Why? Why would someone do something like this after you referred to her a family you have been taking care of for months?

Trying to Understand Why

For months I battled with this, trying to understand why. I tried to talk to her and understand why. She wouldn't meet me or even take my calls. Everything seemed a bit odd. It wasn't until recently that it all made sense. What I never realized was that this person was connected, and good friends with, a few people who liked me the least in town. Can I prove that? No, but that is my "hallucination" of what actually happened when I finally pieced it all together. Does it justify her actions? Of course not. Was it right? Absolutely not. Is there anything I could have done to avoid all of this?

I used to ask myself that question every day, but it wasn't until recently, after fully surrendering my life to Christ and working with my friend, Don, to clear out this gigantic trauma from my mind, that I realized everything that has happened in my life has happened for a reason and could not have happened any other way, period.

God Allows Us to Grow through Hardships

Did God cause any of this? In the past, I would have said yes.

But today I realize that although He didn't cause it, He did allow it. And, better yet, God used the situation to change my life completely.

GOD USED THE SITUATION TO CHANGE MY LIFE COMPLETELY

For months, I was extremely bitter about this whole experience, but now I can clearly see how all the pieces came into play. It needed to happen this way. I couldn't have done anything different after all.

Yes, this family ended up causing us a lot of hurt. They even tried to take legal action against us, but they had no legal standing because we had done everything right from the beginning. So they sought out people affiliated with other YouTube channels who were also bothered by our growth, and they produced an hour-long video so they could tell their side of the story and convince more than two hundred thousand people who didn't know me what a crook I was.

It didn't matter that they couldn't prove anything they were saying. People love drama. That's why TV is such a big deal. People are so empty inside that they are willing to do anything they can to try to fill that void. The situation nearly destroyed me—not my name, my reputation, or even my business. To be honest, I couldn't care less about those things. As a matter of fact, I had already walked away from my business months before any of that had happened. But it nearly destroyed my soul—my mind, will, and emotions. My family was persecuted because of this. We received messages from people we had never met saying that they were going to kidnap my kids. They wanted to hurt my family. They wanted to kill me. That's how bad it was.

I had friends tell me that I should go after my rights, sue this family, and take them for everything they had. For a moment, I really entertained the idea. It wasn't about the money. It never was. It was about making them pay for all the pain they had caused us. I created a video, which has been forever immortalized on the vast internet, not only refuting every single lie they had told and showing proof that we fulfilled our obligations, through emails, contracts, videos, and texts. But only about one hundred thousand people have taken the time to see it. Why? Because as human beings, we are quick to judge. It doesn't matter whether it is right or not. It feels like everyone must voice their opinions, period. They hide behind their computer screens and pass judgment on people they have never met. Wrong? Yes, but what can we do?

God Turns Ashes into Beauty

Jesus told us we need to love our enemies, but how? How do you love someone who is willing to do something like that to you?

That day, my nine-year-old son showed me how. After all, these people were just bullies. Bigger, yes. But still, just bullies. He taught me that hurt people will always hurt people. I do have a choice, though. I chose it to end it with me. I chose to forgive them despite everything they had done. I chose to be thankful for what had happened because that allowed me to understand why I am here. It is what ignited this fire within me to be writing this book today. Can you imagine? God does turn ashes into beauty after all, doesn't He?

Only a few days later, the same week that Matthew told Daniela about the challenges he had been through for two years, was the one-year anniversary of that family posting their video online. And on the day it happened, I decided to send every single person who had been a part of this mess, whether through creating the lie, believing the lie, or even adding wood to the fire, a message telling them that despite everything they had done and whether or not they believed they had done something wrong, I forgave them and was praying that God would bless their lives and care for their families. Most of them didn't respond, of course. They are still hurting in many areas of life, I am sure. Maybe one day we will get a chance to meet and hug this all out, who knows. Maybe not. But in the end, it doesn't even matter.

I forgave them with all my heart. Because it was easy or because I have such a good heart? Neither. Because Jesus first forgave me. Because Daniela forgave me despite all the wrong I had done to her. Because Matthew forgave the bullies at school.

Forgiveness Is the Only Way to Freedom

For an entire year, I couldn't move, literally. My mind was bound because of unforgiveness. I felt like a child who is so wired up and moving all the time that unless someone can tie him to a chair, even if for a moment, he will never be able to sit still and just listen.

I experienced the most excruciating pain I have ever felt. It seemed like my mind was disintegrating little by little. I couldn't put two and two together. Couldn't focus. Hated people. I kept telling myself over and over that I was better off working at a farm with animals instead of with people. I would lie in bed at night and scream inside my head and curse people and their generations to come. I would go into the bathroom, turn off the light, turn on the hot shower, and just sit there with the water gushing over my head, hoping it would all go away. I simply couldn't function. Depression took over in a way I had never experienced before. I started having suicidal thoughts again.

Today I can clearly see why I felt that way. Why I couldn't think straight

159

for an entire year. All He wanted me to do was sit still, listen, and relax for a little bit. All He wanted me to focus on was my family. He wanted to teach me how to be a husband for the first time. How to be a father for the first time. How to be a brother and a friend for the first time. He wanted me to feel what it was like to be a son for the first time. And although I am trying to put this all into words through this book to get you to understand what it felt like, I must be honest and tell you that I don't think I ever will be able to express 100 percent of what it was like.

Throughout this whole time, most of the people who had developed a relationship with us along the years were nowhere to be found. Some of them, with big blogs and even YouTube channels, had the audacity to delete videos and blog posts they had done in partnership with us in the past, which happened to be very lucrative for them at the time, without trying to understand what really happened and without even giving us the benefit of the doubt, for old times' sake. Very few ever reached out to check on us and ask if there was any way they could help. But a few true friends not only reached out but embraced our issue as their own. Although I won't name them here, as I might forget to mention a few, they know exactly who they are. We are forever thankful for their support.

God Is the Only One We Can Really Rely On

God is the only one we can rely on. I don't say any of this because I am still bitter or because I want to see that family one day go through something like what we went through. I wouldn't wish that on anyone.

I say this so you can realize that, although relationships are the main reason we were created, the only one you can really rely on at the end of the day, without a shadow of a doubt and who will never let you down, no matter what happens, is Jesus Christ. He will stand by your side, even through your worst mistakes, and ask the people around you to cast the first stone if they have never done anything wrong their entire lives. That, my friend, is powerful.

In the book of John, a woman who was caught in the act of adultery was dragged before Jesus. The crowd demanded that she be stoned to death for her sin, in accordance with the Law of Moses. Jesus's reply to them applies to situations in our lives today:

They were trying to trap him into saying something they could use against him, but Jesus stooped down and wrote in the dust with his finger. They kept demanding an answer, so he stood up again and said, "All right, but let the one who has never sinned throw the first stone!" (John 8:6–7)

At the time, I didn't realize that even though we were going through the biggest storm we had ever gone through, we were right in the eye of the storm. Nothing was happening to us. We were just fine. Yes, there was a storm, but it was just blowing around us. We were right at the center, where everything was calm. He was taking care of us the whole time. All we needed to do was trust. Really trust Him. He had us in the palm of His hand.

Today I realize how important reading my Bible is. Not as a religious duty that I have to do once a day for thirty minutes and forget all about it throughout the day, but to protect myself against any harm that may come my way. Memorizing Scripture has been key to me because all I have to do is remember His promises, simple as that. If I am walking with Him, His promises will come to pass. I have nothing to worry about.

He will provide the manna as I go through the desert. I don't have to be there for forty years like the Israelites. They were there that long because of their disobedience and unbelief. I have made a commitment to obey and believe, so my journey through the desert needed to last only twelve days—or, in my case, twelve months—when it lasts most people a lifetime. This was enough time for God to take me through the twelve quests we are covering in this book and to fully develop my character in preparation for what was about to come. For that I am forever grateful.

I don't know what is going on in your life today. I don't know who has hurt you in the past. I am sure you have good reasons to feel the way you feel. But I've got to tell you, true and abundant growth will not take place in your life until you choose to forgive—especially if they don't deserve it.

God Purifies Gold by Putting It in the Fire

What God has done in my life has been a true miracle. There is no other way to explain it. Thank God I had already met Larry when this whole thing happened because he was able to guide me through it. I remember calling him through FaceTime, sitting in the room I had

THE ONLY WAY TO PURIFY GOLD IS TO PUT IT IN THE FIRE

rented in Houston, trying to understand why this was all happening. He told me that the only way to purify gold is to put it in the fire. That's what God was doing with us. He was purifying our lives and developing our character so we could get ready for the next phase that was about to start.

If you are going through hell right now, don't stop until you are through it. Surrender your life to Him, and allow Him to finish the good work He has started in your life. I promised you, He will take care of you, too.

But you are a tower of refuge to the poor, O LORD, a tower of refuge to the needy in distress. You are a refuge from the storm and a shelter from the heat. For the oppressive acts of ruthless people are like a storm beating against a wall (Isa. 25:4).

CHAPTER

13

Steps on The Journey
of a Kingsman

Let's review the steps from this chapter that will lead you to your ultimate goal of becoming a Kingsman:

1. Other people can resent your success and try to destroy what you've built out of jealousy. If this happens, turn it over to God, and forgive them. But don't stop striving to honor God with your success.

2. Try to find the lesson God wants to teach you through difficult times.

3. Rely on God to provide you with strength when you feel weak and burdened.

QUEST NINE
GROWTH

CHAPTER 14

Struggling with Purpose

Moving to another country at seventeen years of age, on my own, wasn't the easiest thing on Earth. It was exciting, I admit, but it wasn't simple. I left not only my mother, father, brother, sister, and friends; I also left the love of my life behind. Daniela and I had already been dating for two years and were used to being together all the time, whether it was at school, church, or the gym. We simply loved being together. But we were young and living in our parents' homes, so we had to get creative about finding ways to be alone.

Giving in to Sin Creates an Appetite for More Sin

I mean, what would you expect when you put together two teenagers whose parents are both pastors who spent their lives telling others that most of the things they love doing are wrong? Don't ask me why, but human beings tend to want to do things they aren't supposed to do. It's nothing new. Look at Adam and Eve. They had everything they could ever want, including daily contact with God in the Garden of Eden. He told them they could partake of anything in the Garden except for the fruits from one tree. They defied God's warning and ate from that tree. Why did they feel compelled to have the one thing they weren't supposed to have?

My wife and I did a lot of things we shouldn't have. Premarital sex was one of them. Yes, we knew it was "wrong," but because at times everything seemed to be wrong, we just ended up bundling it all together. What we didn't realize until years down the road was that this "one simple act" would open the door to out-of-control sin that would completely turn our lives upside down.

It wasn't until we heard a sermon by Pastor Robert Morris of Gateway Church that we realized that sin develops in us an appetite that God never intended us to have. Pastor Morris taught us that the things that seemed silly and harmless, such as lying when our parents asked us where we were going, would unleash more negative events in our lives.

What would you expect from two teenagers? Is it surprising that we would tell our parents we were going to do one thing but then really go somewhere private to have sex? After all, we loved each other, and we were going to get married anyway. No harm, no foul, right? Or so we thought. What we understand today but didn't realize at the time is that there is a reason the Bible teaches us what we should and shouldn't do. The appetite that is developed from sneaking around to have sex, which God never intended us to have, will have to be sustained after marriage.

Sinning Makes It More Difficult to Become Satisfied

What do you believe is the problem now? Once you get married, there is no more sneaking around to have sex. It's like an open buffet. You can have all you want. And although it's great, it simply does not satisfy that appetite that was developed earlier. So what do you do now? You must find a way to fulfill it. But it has to be with someone else—someone you can sneak around with and get the same sensation you used to get with your spouse, before you got married.

And now, dear brothers and sisters, one final thing. Fix your thoughts on what is true, and honorable, and right, and pure, and lovely, and admirable. Think about things that are excellent and worthy of praise. Keep putting into practice all you learned and received from me—everything you heard from me and saw me doing. Then the God of peace will be with you (Phil. 4:8–9).

The problem here is that you then end up believing that you no longer love your spouse. That you have nothing in common. That marrying her was the biggest mistake you have ever made. You then divorce her and marry the one you have been sneaking around with, thinking she is the true love of your life. The problem now is that the cycle begins again. Why? Because you no longer need to sneak around to have sex with your new wife. You are back at the buffet, and that appetite you developed is no longer being fulfilled. Make sense?

You see, the enemy—Satan—is not creative. He doesn't have to be. The only real power he has is the power to deceive. He doesn't have to mess with your marriage. If he can just get you to believe that you no longer love your wife because you are no longer having your needs met, he has accomplished his job. Like everything else in this book, I say this from experience. For years, I believed that lie. Why? Was I such a bad person? No. But I had made some bad decisions that led me down a path of self-destruction. The things I partook of in my life in the next few years would get me so hooked, I simply couldn't break free.

To Heal, You Must Surrender and Detox

I often hear people talk about the power that alcohol and drugs have on someone. I have seen it firsthand. My father was an alcoholic, and today I can clearly see how amazing his transformation has been. The challenge I see with some treatment programs is that they assume that you can recover on your own, by following a few steps. The truth is, you can't. At least not in a way that will be truly sustainable. You can't do anything on your own. I know it. I tried to for the longest time.

True transformation and freedom don't come until you fully surrender your life and start going through a detox process. Not in the natural realm like most people believe, but in the spiritual realm, where everything really happens. Have you ever tried to get to a place when you are deaf, dumb, and blind? It is impossible. That is the feeling I had since I was eight years old and was first introduced to pornography. That sin kept me bound for the next twenty-three years. Yes, twenty-three years!

I thank God that I never had to experience the devastating effects of an addiction like alcohol or drugs. But I can tell you for sure that I have felt firsthand the power that sex addiction can have in a human being's life. Pastor Morris used to say that every sin is outward. This one, however, is inward, making it that much more powerful. Have you ever thought about why God tells us to flee from sexual immorality?

Literally run from it? He doesn't want us to stay and fight it because He understands how strong it is.

Run from sexual sin! No other sin so clearly affects the body as this one does. For sexual immorality is a sin against your own body (1 Cor. 6:18).

I Sinned Because I Hated Myself

Most people I have met who have suffered from alcohol and drug addiction turn to these substances to ease some sort of pain, either physical or emotional. I never did anything to ease my pain, or even seek pleasure, believe it or not. My wife is gorgeous, and if you have ever met her, you know exactly what I am talking about. Today I realize that I

I SINNED BECAUSE I WANTED TO HURT MYSELF

sinned because I wanted to hurt *myself*. I hated myself so much, it's hard to even comprehend.

Have you ever met someone who, although he didn't necessarily say it, was prideful and thought he was better than everyone else? That was me. What I realize today is that prideful people have nothing in their hearts but insecurity. They hide behind their money, their businesses, their accomplishments, and anything else they can get their hands on. But deep down, they are very insecure about themselves and feel like they constantly must prove something to someone. Sad, isn't it?

As the years went by, I didn't realize how much my premarital decisions had impacted me. Every time I met with someone to do something I wasn't supposed to, it felt like I had a monster-like creature holding on to me, and when I left, it felt like the creature was gone. I realize today how deceived I was because I was actually trading one for seven, as the saying goes, every time I had another one of those encounters. I went in bad and felt like I came out better, but the reality is that the next day, I felt seven times heavier. No wonder I was losing my mind day after day. There was so much going on that I didn't understand.

I was going through life deaf, dumb, and blind. I remember vividly driving around town for hours, like a zombie, visiting the graveyard to seek some peace; that was the only place I could think of where no one would judge me or say anything. I could just sit there for hours. I would go into a church and lie down in a back pew for hours, asking God to help me because I simply didn't know what to do. I would walk back to my car, shaking because I needed my weekly fix.

For a couple of years, I did give in to those desires, both for pornography and being with other women. The women I chose to hook up with had to be women I had no relationship with. I would just go in, do whatever I wanted, pay, and leave, without ever feeling bad for them.

That soul-crushing appetite for carnal desire consumed me. To try to keep from giving in to my desire for sexual gratification, I would try to satisfy my "appetite" with food. I would drive through two or three fast-food places, grab a bunch of different things, and shove them into my mouth, hoping the sense of self-destruction would go away. But it never worked. I had to have my fix. It was sad to see. Almost pathetic. But what could I do? I was a prisoner. I felt like something was driving me toward destruction. I felt like I had no control. I felt like I was caged within myself, and although I could see what was going on, I couldn't do anything about it.

I know, my God, that you examine our hearts and rejoice when you find integrity there. You know I have done all this with good motives, and I have watched your people offer their gifts willingly and joyously (1 Chron. 29:17).

Trying to Rid Myself of the Demons

At that point, I was a victim after all. I had made some decisions in my past that put me in that situation. Also, the church I grew up in was an ultra-religious, legalistic environment, and it was very difficult at times. I was often reminded that everything I did was a sin, from playing with my friends to wearing a pair of shorts to watching TV. Members of our church would be shunned for doing things the church frowned on.

That constant negative reinforcement of my childhood activities messed with my mind. I got to a point to where I was so messed up that one day I had to get my fix right after a beautiful lunch with my family on Father's Day. Father's Day! Can you imagine?

A few weeks later, I drove all the way to Tampa to see a guy who claimed to be an exorcist because by that time, I actually thought I was possessed. He explained how demons operated and how he could get rid of them. He handed me some materials to read to learn how to deal with demons. Not knowing what else to do, I bought a cross from him so I could keep it in my glove compartment for divine protection. I had no idea what I was doing.

Something within me told me that something was off and I needed help. It is difficult for an addict to seek help, especially if he grew up in an environment where the only thing people knew how to do best was judge and punish.

Is it starting to make sense why the encounter with Larry and the month I spent with him were so impactful? I had never experienced unconditional love from a stranger before. I had a completely twisted view of God. I thought God, church, and religion were all the same thing. Because I had had such a bad experience with the last two, as I got older, developing a relationship with God was last thing I wanted. Why would I want a relationship with someone whose only goal was to punish me? Again, I was deceived.

I Want to Help You Heal, as I Have

I wrote this chapter while sitting in the parking lot of the school that my younger son, Lucca, attends. It was a Friday, and I had finished writing this book seven days earlier. That day, I was supposed to send the final manuscript to my publisher. But I wasn't finished after all. So I sat in the parking lot, retyping this entire chapter on my phone so I could share with you something so personal that I hadn't shared before. I typed for three hours, nonstop. I could barely feel my thumbs by the time I was done. Not because I was trying to hold anything back. As you have noticed throughout this book and as promised in the beginning, I have been more than open with you about my struggles.

Why is that? Why did I feel such a tug in my heart to do this right now?

Because I believe you or someone you care about might be going through something similar to this. Yes, we tend to put on masks to keep everyone thinking everything is good. But is it?

Direct your children onto the right path, and when they are older, they will not leave it (Prov. 22:6).

For months, I roamed around the city of Orlando, sitting in front of churches and mental institutions, unable to move yet understanding that something was wrong. I just didn't know what. I was helpless. I believed the lies for so many years, and those lies became who I was. They became my identity. All I wanted was to take my own life, nothing else. That thought consumed me for years.

But God with His mighty power came into my life, eliminating everything that shouldn't be there and showing me who I really am and what I was created for. It changed me. It changed my life. And it revealed God's purpose for my life.

It can change you too, my friend. It's not too late. But please understand: you have to take the first step. Understand that you can't create lasting change on your own. This all happened to me at the peak of what I thought success was. I had "everything" I needed, yet I had nothing. I wanted to grow. I wanted to find meaning. But for that to happen, a major detox needed to take place. I needed to get everything

YOU CAN'T CREATE LASTING CHANGE ON YOUR OWN

out in the open. I needed to allow God to shine the light in the darkest places. There was no other way.

Feeling the need to surrender, I gave my life to Christ in April 2016. I had not been with another woman for months at that point, but pornography was still a big part of my life. I met Larry four months later, in August, and in October was when we moved to Texas as a family.

But it wasn't until May 2017, when we went to Oklahoma to see a couple of friends who have a beautiful relationship with God—Billy and Beth—that I was completely freed. I finally understood that the reason I didn't have true and complete freedom was because I wasn't asking the right way. I watched a sermon by Joseph Prince in which he said that asking God for help so you can overcome a problem sometimes will do you no good. You need to tell God that you can't do it, even with His help, and tell Him to do it all for you because you can no longer keep going.

Maybe today you are facing similar challenges but have no idea where to go or what to do. Maybe you are struggling to find God's purpose in your own life, and sin is getting in your way. That is exactly how Satan wants it. Here is my advice: get on your knees, look up, cry out for help, and surrender yourself fully to your Creator. Once you do that, get ready. Things are going to get ugly. The enemy is going to try to do anything he can to stop you. But the beauty is that once you are in the center of God's will, nothing can touch you. Your world, like mine, may be turned upside down, but He will keep you still.

You can't grow muscle unless you put stress on it. That's the law of physics. You can't grow unless you give Him the opportunity to get out everything that doesn't belong. Trust me.

God told Moses to keep a journal and document everything as they went through the desert. This is my attempt to do the same.

I want you to have someone to talk to and a place where you can plug in and seek help.

CHAPTER

14

Steps on The Journey of a Kingsman

Let's review the steps from this chapter that will lead you to your ultimate goal of becoming a Kingsman:

1. When tempted to sin, pray to God and resist the urge. Giving in to sin creates an appetite for more sin, which can destroy your life, reputation, and relationships.

2. Recognize that when you sin, it becomes more difficult to satisfy your appetite for the things you should walk away from.

3. To heal, you must surrender your problem or addiction to God and detox.

4. Rely on God and a fellow friend to help you heal.

QUEST TEN
FUN

CHAPTER 15

Enjoying the Ride

It was a hot Texas day. As I sat in my car for a few minutes and looked through my windshield, a crushing sense of anger came over me. As I looked at a group of guys playing all sorts of fun games, I couldn't understand why I did not enjoy the time I was having. Then it finally hit me: that is exactly how I had lived most of my childhood—sitting on the bench, simply watching others play and have fun.

We Are Products of Our Environment

Growing up in a religious, rules-driven environment is the last thing any kid would ever wish for. When my father came to Christ, the entire family followed suit. But it wasn't until a few years later that everyone would realize what a crazy experience that would become. Can you imagine going to church three, four, or even more times a week? Even worse, can you imagine having to tell your wife that going forward, a lot of the things she was used to doing—like shaving any part of her body, for example—would be completely off limits? Can you imagine having to live like that? What about having to remove all the TVs from your home and not being able to wear a pair of shorts because you had always been told that if Jesus came back, you would be left behind?

As I have discussed in previous chapters, whether we want it or not, we all end up being products of our environment. For years, I blamed my father for putting us through this. Only recently I realized that experience was the best possible thing that could have ever happened to him. Was it always healthy or right? No. But it was needed to make the shift that he needed to make and to leave behind the life that was leading him down a dark path so he could start over and one day be able to live out his purpose.

Gateway Church hosts a yearly event called Men's Summit. Thousands of men gather together to worship God, listen to amazing speakers and awesome bands like Switchfoot, eat incredible food, and have a ton of fun. Well, the last part was where I had a bit of a hard time. You see, when we were growing up, we were not allowed to play games. We couldn't play any kind of games because they fostered competition, and the leaders of the church did not think competition was healthy or godly. So my siblings and I were not allowed to participate in any of it.

We used to attend a Christian school back in my home town in Brazil, Maringá. Every afternoon after class, the kids would start a friendly soccer match. My father usually would arrive at the school a little while after our classes were over, which gave us a bit of time to just sit and wait because we knew that joining in the game would get us in a lot of trouble.

So, after going to lunch that day at the Men's Summit and parking my car, you can only imagine some of the memories that came into my mind as I sat there watching everyone play and have a good time. Everyone but me.

The night before, right after the event, some of my friends invited me over to join in some of the games they were playing outside the church. I couldn't get myself to play. I sat on the sidelines as they asked me to come join them. I came up with excuses for why I shouldn't play, not understanding why at thirty-two years of age, I was having such a hard time. Little did I know that the next day, everything would make a lot of sense.

Despite What We Were Taught, We Need to Show Our Emotions

One of the great things about events like these, because they are created specifically for guys, is that we get to express ourselves in a way most men would never think about doing if their wives and kids were sitting next to them.

At the Men's Summit, there is a major focus on working through the emotional issues we all build up throughout our lives. The pastors want to make sure no one leaves the same way they came in. Because we are told our entire lives that, as men, we need to be tough and not show your emotions, we end up building up a wall that will get us in a lot of trouble later on. For the rest of our lives, we have a tough time showing our emotions, even when they are appropriate. Hiding our emotions gives the people around us, especially our families, the impression that we simply lack emotions, which couldn't be further from the truth. I know this from experience because for a long time, I had the hardest time showing my wife any type of emotion. I didn't know why. All I knew was, that was how I was built, and no matter what happened, I simply could not change.

Rewriting the Script

When you go through certain experiences, you end up believing lies that make absolutely no sense and nearly drive you to madness. I wasn't mentally tortured by someone; that's not what I mean. But when you are exposed to things that no eight-year-old should ever be exposed to, such as demon-possessed people foaming up from the mouth at 2:00 a.m., day in and day out, that tends to mess with your mind a bit.

Why am I bringing all this up? Because this has been an area that I have to constantly work in. Simply having fun is a very new concept to me. While everyone else is enjoying the ride that is this wonderful life God gave us, I am still sitting on the sidelines. Because the disdain for fun was engrained into me so deeply, I am still trying to overcome it. Having fun seems like wasting time to me. Whenever I think about just taking some time off and not being productive, that nearly drives me to madness. Some of my friends find it hard to believe that whenever I am asked what I like to do for fun, the answer I usually give them is that I like to work. It is hard to admit this, but I wouldn't be honest if I gave them a different answer.

Now, imagine how something like this plays out when you have two little boys like I do. Not very good, is it? I have to push myself to do an activity with them every time we are about to do something that remotely resembles having fun. But like everything else in life, especially when it comes to them, I want to be as intentional as I possibly can.

WE FOLLOW THE SCRIPTS THAT HAVE BEEN WRITTEN FOR US

When we are children, we do what our parents expect of us without question. We follow the scripts that have been written for us by the adults who are raising us. But those scripts don't always align with God's plan for our lives. This means we have to rewrite the script and learn to do what God expects of us and is good for us.

Again, my father did the best he could with what he had. He never allowed us to go without anything. He was always a great provider; for that I am forever thankful. I am going to spend the rest of my life doing my very best for my kids so they can do the best for their kids as well, even if that means stepping out of my comfort zone and breaking through my personal issues.

My wife always tells me to find a hobby—anything that will get my mind off things. I have taken tae kwon do, started going to the gym, gone wakeboarding, snowboarding, bowling, skydiving, and ridden motorcycles. I have taken some golf lessons and even joined a group to learn how to make Kombucha tea and other natural things. But nothing seems to stick. Golf has been the one activity that, with a little bit of effort, I have been focusing on—mainly because I heard that the best deals happen on the golf course, if you know what I mean.

Always be full of joy in the Lord. I say it again—rejoice! Let everyone see that you are considerate in all you do. Remember, the Lord is coming soon.

Don't worry about anything; instead, pray about everything. Tell God what you need, and thank him for all he has done. Then you will experience God's peace, which exceeds anything we can understand. His peace will guard your hearts and minds as you live in Christ Jesus (Phil. 4:4-7).

Being Aware of an Issue Is the First Step to Healing

This is one area I have been giving a lot of thought lately. As I have mentioned throughout this book, the first step to being able to solve an issue is to become aware of it. Without self-awareness, no matter how much people say you need to fix something, it will never be at the top of your priority list. You know something is wrong when you are a having a hard time picking up the bicycle you have just bought your nine-year-old to teach him how to ride, and all of a sudden, your breathing becomes labored and anxiety is consuming you, and you haven't even started moving yet.

Recently, I started working with my friend, Don. Most of us allow past traumas to dictate how we live our lives. This is one truth that has affected my life quite a bit. Unless I am willing to do something about it, it will never change. I love the results I am getting with the process God has put me through, but I also understand that this is a journey of healing. It will take some time and effort on my part.

Don says that our subconscious mind is like computer software—designed to function at full capacity. The challenge is that past traumas are like error messages—no matter how much you ignore them, they simply won't go away. You have to find and eliminate the error before the software can go back to functioning the way it was intended to work.

I have seen so many wins in my life already since starting this process of eliminating the impact that past traumas have had on my current life. I know for a fact I am about to have a breakthrough in this area. It is important to me because I want to make sure that my kids have amazing memories of us having fun together. I am all about breaking generational curses that end up influencing our family, and that is one of them. But first, I had to be aware of these generational curses and the negative impact they have had on me.

Always Continue Growing, Learning, and Improving

I currently live in Orlando, and you probably know what we have in our backyard—yes, Disney World®. We live about fifteen minutes away from Disney, so you can imagine what it must be like to have two young boys, live that close to Disney, and have to muster the courage and enthusiasm to venture out to another day at Magic Kingdom for the kids' sake. My wife, Daniela, on the other hand, simply loves Disney, for which I am very thankful. When my older son, Matthew, was about four years old, we ended up buying annual passes to Disney, so Daniela and he were there pretty much every week, enjoying the rides. Me? Not so much. I still made it once a month, but it was not my favorite pastime.

This was five years ago, so a lot has improved since then. I keep on saying that Walt Disney has definitely cracked the code to success. Think about it: Where else do you find a place where adults become kids, pay more than $100 a day to visit the park, and are willing to stand in line for one hour or more under a sun that is burning up at 100 degrees to enjoy a thirty-second ride and can hardly wait to do it all over again for multiple days? That, my friend, is what you can call an amazing success story.

See? That's my fun—analyzing things—and even though most people may find it extremely boring, my fun when I go to Disney World is to find out how many people went through the park that day at $100 per head and how many of them have bought $3 bottles of water and $15 cheeseburgers so I can try to figure out how much revenue the park brought in that day. Go figure.

I am sharing this with you because we all have our struggles. Remember? This is a journey—the Journey of a Kingsman—and I don't believe the journey ever ends. We try. We improve. We try harder. We grow continually. But I believe there is a reason it never ends. Think about those astronauts who have been to the moon and back. What do they have to look forward to after being to the moon? Nothing else can ever compare. No wonder some of them suffer from depression for the rest of their lives. They literally have nothing to look forward to—or do they?

I never want to stop growing, learning, and becoming better. Maybe I am struggling a little in this area today, but when I look back, I can clearly see how much progress I have already made. I can clearly see that I have grown—that I am getting better each day. That excites me. It excites my family. It excites us because this journey called life is all about constant growth and improvement.

Instruct the wise, and they will be even wiser. Teach the righteous, and they will learn even more (Prov. 9:9).

It's about finding your purpose and fulfilling your calling. But even that can become a burden if you don't know how to go about it the right way. Have you ever seen someone live out his dream career, only to see his family fall apart because he is traveling all the time? Or stand at the pulpit and preach a beautiful message about marriage and family, only to come home and face his wife and kids, and realize he is not walking the talk? I have been there. I know the feeling, and I've got to tell you—I never want to go back. It's too painful. As a Kingsman, you will need to eventually find your God-given purpose and then live it out every day, for the rest of your life, that is, if you ever want to be truly fulfilled in life.

Live Intentionally, and Be Grateful

Living intentionally is an amazing way to live. When you begin being intentional about the big things—your family, your purpose, your spirit, and your soul—and even the little things such as your fun time, your entire life changes. To be intentional means to define your purpose in life and then to make sure every action you take and every word you speak aligns with that purpose. It means that we don't allow our past environment or bad influences to drive our actions.

Maybe you have, like me, had some trouble in this area because of bad past experiences, but don't let that hold you back. Follow the advice in the old adage, and stop along the way to smell the roses. Learn how to appreciate every little blessing in your life. Start being thankful to

BE GRATEFUL FOR THE CIRCUMSTANCES YOU HAVE GONE THROUGH

everything and everyone around you. Be grateful for the circumstances you have gone through and the ones you are currently going through. They happened for a reason and couldn't have happened any other way. They developed you into the person you are today.

If you are sitting in your car watching other people play and feeling anger trying to take over, push through it. Decide today you will not accept this. Your past does not equal your future. You can change it. God is right there with you, and so am I. You have an entire community of like-minded individuals just waiting to help you break through and enjoy the ride.

CHAPTER

15

Steps on The Journey
of a Kingsman

Let's review the steps from this chapter that will lead you to your ultimate goal of becoming a Kingsman:

1. Acknowledge that you are a product of your environment and that the guidance you received as a child doesn't necessarily align with God's plan for you.

2. Be aware of issues that are keeping you from living the life God intended for you.

3. "Rewrite the script" to move forward, as necessary, replacing lessons you learned long ago with the truth of God's Word.

4. Show your emotions, even though you have probably always been taught that you shouldn't do so.

5. Know that being aware of an issue or problem is the first step in resolving it and healing from it.

6. Always continue learning, growing, and improving.

7. Live intentionally, making sure that every action you take and every word you speak aligns with your God-given purpose.

8. Be grateful for everything, even your hardships, because they are molding you into the person of character God wants you to be.

QUEST ELEVEN

TIME

CHAPTER 16

An Effective Strategy

"Time heals all wounds." Have you heard this statement before?

For a long time, I believed it. But to be honest, I no longer believe life works that way. This is like saying that knowledge is power. There is also something wrong with that. *Applied* knowledge is power—there needs to be *application* for the knowledge to do anything. Time heals wounds, yes, but only when the wounds have been treated. With time, exposed wounds that haven't been cared for will only attract unwanted things—and more pain.

I believe that to live according to your God-given purpose, you need an effective strategy—not just any strategy, but one based on your unique talents, situation, and life goals.

Live by Design, Not by Default

Time is the only real asset we have that we can never get more of. And even though it is the most valuable asset we have, some of us go through life basically giving it away as if it isn't worth anything.

> TIME IS THE ONLY REAL ASSET WE HAVE THAT WE CAN NEVER GET MORE OF

I talk often about living life by design and not by default. The reason I put so much emphasis on this is because for too many years, I lived my life by default. What I didn't realize was that because there was no true intention, my life was just a part of someone else's design.

That influenced many areas of my adventure. Pornography stole a huge part of my life. It robbed me of great moments. It cheated me of deep connections. As I mentioned before, I was first introduced to pornography when I was only eight years old by someone really close. What I didn't realize at the time was that my exposure to that dark world would cause a great deal of pain in my life, rob me of so many amazing blessings, and develop an appetite God never intended me to have.

We all want God to do things we think are right. Or things that feel right. It wasn't until recently that I was finally able to get a good grasp on why He does what He does, when He does it. It's for our own good. Solomon said it best:

For everything there is a season,

a time for every activity under heaven.

A time to be born and a time to die.

A time to plant and a time to harvest.

A time to kill and a time to heal.

A time to tear down and a time to build up.

A time to cry and a time to laugh.

A time to grieve and a time to dance.

A time to scatter stones and a time to gather stones.

A time to embrace and a time to turn away.

A time to search and a time to quit searching.

A time to keep and a time to throw away.

A time to tear and a time to mend.

A time to be quiet and a time to speak.

A time to love and a time to hate.

A time for war and a time for peace.

(Eccl. 3:1–8)

This freed me up in a major way.

Why? Because I kept trying to figure out why things were happening. Why was I going through this mess? Why was all this happening to me? Understanding that there is a time, a season, for everything was liberating. Imagine having twelve months of summer or twelve months of winter. Or even twelve months of fall or spring. Imagine if the sun never set or the moon never showed up. What if time sat still and nothing or no one ever grew older as time went by? Can you imagine how boring that would be?

Most of us don't think about things like this constantly, if ever. I do. All the time. And yes, sometimes it nearly drives me insane. But I have learned to accept it. I have learned to appreciate it. After all, there is a reason He made me this way. Because everything He does has a purpose, a design. I actually get excited now when I wake up each morning because that might be, as they say, when the light bulb finally comes on and He gets to reveal to me something amazing that I never thought possible. Who knows, that might be today.

Time Maximizes Your Current Situation

Do you ever stop to think and even say things like, "Where has time gone? Time flies! Boy, I am getting old." Or do you ever look in the mirror and wonder in awe, "How on Earth did I get here?"

It was my thirtieth birthday. I was at the peak of what I thought defined success, at least compared to the reality I grew up in. I had everything I could possibly want: a beautiful wife by my side, two amazing sons, a gorgeous home, two very nice cars, a successful multimillion-dollar business, and a million-dollar net worth. What else could I possibly want by the time I was thirty? I wasn't born with a silver spoon in my mouth. I had fought hard to be where I was.

My wife put together a beautiful party and invited about a hundred friends over to celebrate it with us. I remember it vividly. There was so much good food and an open bar. Great music and beautiful decor. Everyone was having a great time. It was a beautiful night as we looked down from the eighteenth floor at the well-lit buildings all around us at the Citrus Club in downtown Orlando.

On the outside, the evening appeared to be a great success. On the inside, from my view? Nothing but a great void. As I looked at my reflection in a tall window, I couldn't help but wonder if I had really accomplished all I set out to accomplish by the time I was thirty.

When I first moved by myself to the United States, I was working as a busboy. For a couple of years, I had already been dating the beautiful lady who is now my wife. But I left her back in Brazil with the promise that I would go to America, work as much as I could to gather enough money, and go back home so we could start our lives together. Start our lives together in Brazil we did indeed—just didn't stay there for very long. Daniela and I ended up marrying when I was eighteen years old. We had a rough start.

After I had lived in the United States for a year, I returned to Brazil, and Daniela and I got married that same month—November. Our plan was to move to the States the following month, in December. Things didn't work out with our visas, so we stayed in Brazil for about a year. We both felt frustrated, and had some pretty nasty verbal fights. We lived with my parents for the first six months after we got married because we were still trying to get our visas. After a while we figured we wouldn't be able to get the visas anytime soon after all, so she and I moved into a small apartment. Was everything OK? No. That's when things got really bad. We actually came very close to getting divorced that first year.

A few months later, we were finally able to get our visas and move to Colorado to start our life together. Like most couples, we had our ups and downs. We worked like crazy to build a comfortable nest egg for three years so we could move back to Brazil, start school, buy a house, have a baby, and enjoy a life that would look a lot like the lives we had always seen the people around us live. We did work hard for three years, but we never moved back to Brazil.

I have always been told that it's easy to get used to good things. That's not where the problem normally lies; the challenge is getting used to things that are not so good.

Although it may seem that time can be a faithful friend when you are living according to God's Word and under His guidance, and a cruel thing when you are not, my experience has been that time is a lot like money—it is neutral. It isn't good or bad. It is, however, a maximizer. It maximizes the way you feel about your current situation—if you are unhappy, time maximizes your misery, and if you are happy, time maximizes your joy and contentment.

Have you ever done any type of work or other activity that you enjoyed so much that you didn't realize time had passed? It seems like only about an hour has passed, when you finally look at your watch and realize that five hours have rushed by? At the same time, have you ever stood in line or sat in traffic for five minutes, and it seemed like an eternity? Isn't it funny how time works?

Abide by God's Timing

Sometimes, when we pray to God to change our situations, we become impatient and frustrated. But God acts according to the timeline that is appropriate for the plan He has for your life.

Pastor Rick Warren of Saddleback Church preached a sermon titled "Daring Faith: Daring to Wait on God." Many of his points hit me as I was thinking about this time quest:

> Technology has made us more impatient. There are some things we only learn through waiting. An immature child does not know the different between "no" and "not yet." Our inability to wait is the

cause of so many problems in our lives. Have you ever been in a hurry when God wasn't? Waiting is not passivity; you do all you can to get ready. You get prepared and act as though you already have it. When waiting, don't sit around passively doing nothing. Waiting is the time you develop the skills and habits you use later. Never be lazy in your work but serve the Lord enthusiastically. You have been waiting on God but God has been waiting on you to demonstrate faith.[1]

Throughout this book, my goal has been to help you understand purpose better and gain an even better idea of how to pursue that purpose. One of the main reasons I decided to focus on this topic is because of the importance purpose plays in our lives, especially when it relates to time. We all have twenty-four hours in a day. That's 1,440 minutes and 86,400 seconds. Whether you agree with it, or whether it feels that way to you or not, a lot of time is placed in our hands. It's kind of like a teacher who starts off the year telling his students that they all start with an A-plus, and their only job is to make sure they keep it that way throughout the year by putting the things they are learning to good use. God expects us to use the time He gives us wisely.

Design Your Life to Control Your Own Time

One of my favorite movies is a film called *In Time*. It's a 2011 American science fiction, action thriller film starring Justin Timberlake. The story takes place in the near future, and what people know as currency today is no longer valid; time is the new currency. People steal, kill, and kidnap each other, but what they are looking for is to simply have more time on Earth. They buy, sell, and trade things based on time. Everything revolves around time. There are banks and pawnshops where people can make loans and trade things for time. The rich have a lot of time, and the poor have very little. Does this sound familiar?

1. "Waiting on God," sermon notes, Grace Baptist Church, Oroville, California, http://www.graceoroville.org/.

The movie starts when the mother of the main character, played by Timberlake, dies because she "timed out." He then sets out on a journey to avenge his mother's death and take on those who manipulated the system. The reason I bring this up is because, in my opinion, this movie shows our current reality. You see, when the people in the movie go to work, they get credited time that allows them to buy things, eat, and live.

How is that different from how most people live today? Their bosses dictate which part of town they are going to live in, what kind of car they are going to drive, where their kids will go to school, how often they get to eat out, and the quality of clothes they get to wear. You may think I am completely out of my mind, but think about it for a second. By dictating how much your employers pay you on an hourly basis, they are telling you how much your time is worth. Therefore, they are automatically dictating how you will live your life.

Back when slavery was abolished, people were very excited because they were finally free. Or were they? What they didn't realize is that the only difference now is that they are getting paid for doing the work they were doing without pay before. Their bosses still dictate how they are going to live their lives based on what they are paying them. Not only that, but their bosses also dictate when they can eat, when they can go to the restroom, when they have to come in, when they have to leave, and even when, and if, they get to take any time off. Now, tell me, doesn't this sound a lot like slavery to you? A more legalized and humanized type of slavery, yes, but slavery nevertheless. Their bosses own them after all, even if only for one-third of their day.

Don't get me wrong. I want you to be thankful for where God has placed you and how He is using your professional role to provide you with means for your family. But to reach your full God-given potential, it's important for you to spend your time doing the things you enjoy and that align with your life purpose.

Take a moment to rate your level of fulfillment and happiness on a scale of one to five. One means you are extremely unfulfilled and have to drag yourself to work every day and five means you have such an overwhelming sense of excitement about your job that you can barely wait for Monday to come so you can go back to work and fulfill another day in the destiny God has created for you.

Spend Every Moment Wisely

I am a big fan of investing and entrepreneurship. These two things are what God used in my life to allow me to go through what I have experienced these past two years without it being a burden on my family financially. I can't even imagine what it would have been like if I were still working a job and having to go through all of this at the same time. I am so thankful for the opportunity to pretty much take two years off work and still be able to live an amazing lifestyle. This is because I had a business that was operating without me for the first year and investments that supported us in the last part of the journey.

The last thing I want you to feel here is any type of guilt, condemnation, or even resentment for being where you are. All I want is for you to

> SOMETHING MIGHT NEED TO CHANGE BEFORE YOU CAN EXPERIENCE THE FREEDOM OF TIME AND MONEY

understand that something might need to change before you can experience the freedom of time and money you are looking for so you can pursue your God-given calling. From my experience, it will not happen until you start understanding the importance that time has in your life and what a phenomenal gift it is when your Creator deposits another 86,400 seconds into your life account every day at midnight.

Follow God's Amazing Plan for Your Life

As I discussed in the wealth chapter, your ultimate goal when it comes to your financial life should be to develop enough passive income as soon as possible to meet and exceed your expenses to free you up completely so you can pursue your God-given calling. And I don't mean by the time you are in your sixties, like most people think. I mean when you are in the prime of your life. I believe you can absolutely achieve this in ten years or less—if you have a solid strategy in place and if you are willing to step out of your comfort zone and do whatever it takes to achieve your goals. This endeavor has to be good not only for you but also for the people around you, and it has to be moral, legal, and ethical, of course.

If I had known these strategies when I was thirty, I could have retired then. Not retired in the way that most people think about retirement. I love the work I am doing today. What I mean is that I would have been able to create enough passive income in the past ten years to be able to give my family and me a great lifestyle for the rest of our lives. I said "a great lifestyle"—not just being able to pay the bills like most people when they retire. That is the power of an effective life strategy.

My prayer is that you come to a place of such clarity in your life that you decide once and for all that you will not allow anyone or anything to dictate how you are going to live. Follow God's direction. He has an amazing plan for you. He knows exactly where you should be investing that precious time He has given you. He wants you to do so much more.

You are amazing—uniquely created for a purpose. Allow God to do the good work He started in you.

CHAPTER

16

Steps on The Journey of a Kingsman

Let's review the steps from this chapter that will lead you to your ultimate goal of becoming a Kingsman:

1. Live by design, not by default.

2. Abide by God's timing.

3. Design your life to control your own time.

4. Spend every moment wisely.

5. Be willing to listen and follow His call for your life.

6. Decide to change and to follow your dreams.

7. Keep in mind that time is the only thing you cannot get back, so cherish every moment as if it were your last.

8. Ask for direction on how you should be spending every minute of your day.

9. Have good strategies in place so life doesn't just sneak up on you.

10. Be intentional about every part of your day.

11. Don't allow people to pull you into their agendas.

12. Follow an effective strategy to live according to God's plan.

QUEST TWELVE
DREAM

CHAPTER 17

Living By Design

If you could have the ideal life, what would that look like?

I mean, if you could just snap your fingers right now and have your life look exactly how you see it in your wildest dreams, who would you be? Where would you be? Who would you be with? What kind of work would you be doing? How much money would you be making? What kind of home would you have? What kind of car would you be driving? What would your bank account look like?

Better yet, what would your relationship with your wife and kids look like? What would your relationship with your Creator be like? Who would be experiencing this journey with you, mentoring you, encouraging you, helping you? Who would you be mentoring, encouraging, helping? What kind of impact would you want to cause in the world? What would you do with your time?

Most People Have No Idea What They Want

Through the years, I have had the opportunity to meet thousands of people from all ages, races, religions, and nationalities. I have met employees and self-employed individuals as well as business owners and investors, and they all had one thing in common: If given unlimited resources and time, most of them had no idea what they would want their lives to look like. I don't mean the typical overall picture of what an ideal life would look like. And surely not the type of life you see on TV. I mean an actual detailed plan of what the perfect life would look like. I believe that is the reason most people never achieve abundance on Earth—they don't know how or even what to ask for. They have no plan, strategy, or design for their lives.

Not too long ago, I had a revelation and really believe in my heart that it was God-inspired. I felt Him speaking to my heart as I was going through one of my biggest struggles in life—trying to understand who I was and what I was created for. I prayed over and over for Him to reveal His purpose for my life and to show me what He had in mind when He created me. I was tired of living how I had been living up until that point—by my own design but with no direction, not understanding what the true purpose of free will really meant. As I prayed about it, I could clearly see in my mind the picture of a white canvas and someone handing me a brush, telling me to design my life exactly how I would like it to be. I also felt God speak to my heart and say, "The reason you don't get what you want is because you don't know how to ask!"

I know this might seem a little silly at first and even a little selfish. I know we are not supposed to be living life by our design, but by His. The moment that thought hit me, though, I felt something stronger saying, "And who do you believe gave you the ability to dream the life you have been dreaming about?"

Finding Your Purpose Doesn't Have to Be Complicated

That really struck me. It made complete sense. Think about it. From the moment I submit my will entirely to my Creator and ask Him to teach me how to think, feel, and act, everything that comes into my mind that is good for me, as well as for the people around me, that is legal, moral, and ethical, must also come from Him.

I had watched many long videos with messages delivered by pastors and speakers, trying to understand the formula for finding my purpose on Earth. It wasn't until I watched a three-minute video by Evangelist Daniel Kolenda that I realized we make finding our purpose in life—that one thing we were called to do—way too complicated. We also make designing our lives exactly the way we want to live way too complex. After all, He made me. He knit me in my mother's womb. He knows me better than anyone on this Earth. So if I am dreaming about the ideal life and I am living within His will, I believe I can go after it and victory will be mine.

Now, I am not naïve enough to think that simply because I want it, everything will magically happen. As I mentioned before, God will do His 99 percent of the work as long as I do my 1 percent. It's also important to remember that nothing will happen on my timing, but according to His perfect timing.

Trust in the Lord and do good. Then you will live safely in the land and prosper. Take delight in the Lord, and he will give you your heart's desires. Commit everything you do to the Lord. Trust him, and he will help you. He will make your innocence radiate like the dawn, and the justice of your cause will shine like the noonday sun. Be still in the presence of the Lord, and wait patiently for him to act. Don't worry about evil people who prosper or fret about their wicked schemes (Ps. 37:3–6).

Surrender Your Life to God's Design

Why are we constantly afraid of everything and everyone around us? I was there not too long ago. But I can tell you that the truth set me free. Now I understand that my spirit is perfect because it looks just like the spirit that raised Jesus from the dead. When I finally understood that, I realized I can do all things in Him because He gives me strength. Do you understand how amazing that is? It changes everything. He's got my back. He's got your back. Always. No matter what.

I used to think surrendering my life's design to God would imprison me and not allow me to live the life I wanted to live. But it is really the complete opposite. This new phase of my life has been completely incredible because I have finally surrendered.

As I think about my past, I can't help but notice how much of a prisoner I was. How do people do it? How do they go through an entire life never being able to experience this freedom? How did I do it? I would hear people preach the Gospel and tell myself I would never want to follow God's will. For the most part, the people preaching those messages lived a life different from the God they talked about. Not only that, but they did it in a way that was absolutely condemning and that drove people away from a life of redemption and purpose.

Lead by Example

When I first met Larry, I realized that "preaching the Gospel" was nothing more than sharing my story. It was about telling others what Jesus did for me and what He did for them on the cross. I love my life, and I love talking about what He did for me. Why, then, did I have such a hard time with this before? I can summarize it in one word: transformation— or a lack thereof. I had never experienced true transformation until I got down on my knees that one day at my house.

I viewed these people as used-car salesmen who didn't really believe in their products. Have you ever seen someone who works at the Chevy dealership but drives a Ford? What's wrong with that picture? I don't know about you, but I have always believed in leading by example. I can't tell you to do something, or even "sell" you something, if I don't fully own it and believe in it. When I sold vacation homes, I owned vacation homes. When I talk about taking control of your finances, it is because I have taken control of my finances first. When I talk about living a balanced life, it is because I live a balanced life. Do you get what I am saying?

I still get a chance to meet a lot of people on a daily basis, and the first thing I like to do is ask them about their lives, their goals, and their aspirations. Sometimes I get a few weird looks, as if they are trying to tell me, "I barely know you." Or "Don't you think this sort of conversation is a little too deep?" But to be honest, I don't care. I once heard someone say that you are the average of the five people you spend the most time with, and I believe nothing could be further from the truth. The way I see it, if I am going to invest any time in this relationship, I need to make sure it will be profitable for both of us.

Again, I am a numbers guy, so everything is about return on investment. I don't mean financial return necessarily, but I do want to make sure that we are not wasting each other's time and that the "transaction" will be beneficial for both of us.

I love talking to people who think outside the box:

- People who really believe they were created for so much more.
- People who believe they are uniquely blessed with specific gifts and talents.
- People who believe they were created by an amazing God and placed on this Earth to fulfill an amazing mission, a true purpose in life.

Nothing bores me more than someone who does not want to talk about their goals, their dreams, and the impact they want to have in the world but want instead to talk about the weather or why I believe they should get a red car instead of a blue one. My grandmother used to say, "If you don't have anything good to say, don't say anything at all." I live by this principle. Even though it might give certain people the wrong impression, I always stick with it.

WHAT WOULD YOUR IDEAL LIFE LOOK LIKE?

Define What Your Ideal Life Looks Like

Again, I am going to challenge you: What would your ideal life look like? I would love it if you would share it with us in our online community sometime soon. But, in the meantime, I am going to share with you a little bit of what my ideal life would look like.

What My Ideal Life Looks Like

As I am writing this book, the year 2017 is ending. My wife, Daniela, and I have two amazing sons: Matthew, who is nine, and Lucca, who is three. They are incredible, and we love them dearly. But because Daniela and I both grew up with two other siblings, we would love to have a third child. We haven't decided yet whether we are going to go the natural route or maybe even adopt, but a third child is definitely a strong possibility.

My wife is an amazing interior designer. She is the first in both our families to get her bachelor's degree from an American school, so I am extremely proud of her. She has designed more than three hundred homes in the past four years, so she has had quite a bit of experience. But her work consumes a lot of her time. I know how important family is to her, so one of my goals is to be able to support our family 100 percent so she can scale her work down a bit. Now again, when I say "support our family," I don't mean just pay the bills. I shared with you some about the financial successes we had since we started to change the way we think. It has been an absolute blessing. We have gone from being employees to being self-employed to owning our own business, and that was a lot of fun. But it has its limitations.

One of the biggest goals I am currently working toward is to build a clientele of successful people whom I can help build an effective financial strategy so they can free up their time by creating passive income that exceeds their expenses every month. I don't need a lot of clients because the work I do is so specific and hard to find. But I do want to make sure I can work with these clients from anywhere in the world. Because of the knowledge base I have built in the financial services arena in the past eight years, I can show them exactly how to be 100 percent free financially in ten years or less, instead of in the typical forty years it takes most people.

Why am I sharing this with you? Because when we talk about the ideal life, you must understand all the details. Having a high income is awesome, but if it takes up all your time, then what good does that do you and your family? Daniela and I want to take the kids to a different country every year starting next year, to spend one month during the summertime immersed in a different culture and learn a different language, without having to worry about money. Sounds pretty cool, right?

The other eleven months out of the year, we plan on spending where we currently live—Orlando, Florida—mentoring other couples and helping them overcome the obstacles we overcame. We plan to buy a beautiful home and replicate what Larry and Devi have been doing

GOD HAS ALLOWED US TO GO THROUGH WHAT WE WENT THROUGH FOR A REASON

back in Texas. I believe God has allowed us to go through what we went through for a reason. We believe every experience we have lived through didn't happen by chance. Every lesson we have learned will have been a waste of time unless we can share it with others so they, too, can have an amazing breakthrough. We want to bring these couples to spend a weekend at our house once a month so we can spend quality time with them and teach them how to replicate this strategy back in their hometowns. We are really excited about this project.

We both also plan on traveling all around, but we still want to be able to focus on our kids, sharing with others what God has done in our lives. We see how Larry and Devi live their lives and how much God uses them to impact the lives of so many other people. It lights us up. We want to be able to do our part.

Let Your Imagination Run Wild

Can you imagine a world like this? Where people are not bound to their nine-to-five jobs or their businesses and can travel the world sharing their stories about how God has completely changed their lives? I don't know about you, but that would be extremely exciting for me.

Impossible? Yes, if you believe in your mind that it is.

The reason I wanted to share with you a little bit about our plans is so you can realize that the sky is not the limit. Imagine utopia for a second. Imagine that are no limits. Imagine your life could be painted exactly how you would want it to be.

Why? Because your Creator has planted big dreams in you. He wants to see those dreams coming to fruition. I say, "I want you to imagine" because your subconscious mind does not understand time and space. To your subconscious mind, everything is happening right now, and anything is possible. It cannot tell the difference between fantasy and reality. This isn't just a bunch of hype, trust me. This is science. This is how your mind is built. This is what I have been experiencing most of my life. Now, will all of our plans come to fruition exactly the way we want them to? Probably not. And I say this because God has much bigger plans for us than our little minds will ever be able to comprehend, and that excites me even more than getting what is expected.

So my challenge to you today is to let your imagination run wild. Let God show you why He created you. Live by design—His design. Let Him show you the big dreams He has uploaded to your "software." Let Him show you how He can use your life to be an inspiration to the people around you so they, too, can live out the life that He intended for you to live when He created you.

CHAPTER

17

Steps on The Journey
of a Kingsman

Let's review the steps from this chapter that will lead you to your ultimate goal of becoming a Kingsman:

1. Picture your life as a blank canvas on which you can design it however you like. Define what every aspect of your ideal life looks like.

2. Let that vision reveal your God-given purpose.

3. Let your imagination run wild.

4. Surrender your life to God's design.

5. Lead by example.

6. Live your life by design, not by default, and work on achieving your optimum use of the quests in this book: purpose, spirit, soul, body, relationships, family, wealth, contribution, growth, fun, time, and dreams.

One night, I took a three-hour walk. I was extremely frustrated because I wanted so badly for God to show me what He wanted me to do with my life. I had just gotten back from Texas a couple of months earlier and was still completely lost regarding what I should do for work and with my life overall. Should I go back to real estate? Insurance? Should I start another company? Should I go to work for someone else?

I wished so badly that I had a mentor in that area who could guide me along the way. Someone I could call and grab a cup of coffee with, explain what I was going through, and maybe get some insight. But I didn't have anyone. That's when it dawned on me that most people go through life like this. They are messed up, going through life deaf, dumb, and blind and doing things they shouldn't do to fill a void that never gets filled. If they could only talk to someone who would understand them and guide them along the way.

And the name came to me: The Kingsman Academy. A mixture of the support and guidance I wish I had experienced while growing up. A place where people can mentor and be mentored to live lives that honor our King, Jesus Christ. Where we can find out what part of the "body" we were created to be. And once we are fully developed, we can train others to be the best part of the body they can be as well.

Being a Kingsman is what allows us to live life how God intended us to live. Mastering the twelve quests s not optional. It is a must if we ever want to reach the level of fulfillment we have been looking for our entire lives. To be able to live a balanced life, always, regardless of our circumstances.

How would we act and behave if we were always in the presence of the King? How would we deal with each area of our lives (quests)? Would we do enough just to get by, or would we do everything we could to be the best we can be?

Imagine a royal child. Imagine the way he or she is brought up. Imagine the things the child is taught. He or she is always being shaped to be royalty.

That's how I view us. We are called to lead our families to a Fantastic Destiny. We were called to rule the Earth. But how can we do that? Most people are grown-up children. They are bigger and have better toys, but they are still children.

The Kingsman Academy is a movement of like-minded individuals with a shared vision, shared mission, and shared purpose to live their

> THE KINGSMAN ACADEMY IS A MOVEMENT OF LIKE-MINDED INDIVIDUALS WITH A SHARED VISION, MISSION, AND PURPOSE

lives by the highest standards and, as a result, have the highest possible level of influence on those around them.

Please don't think that joining me and other individuals on this journey is about being perfect. God knows we are all flawed, broken, and, candidly, messed up. We get beaten up and sometimes even knocked down, but I have news for you: we don't have to stay down! By supporting one another on our respective life journeys as we all discover and follow God's plan for our lives, we can achieve more than we ever dreamed.

1. Assess how happy you are right now. What needs to change?

2. Imagine being driven by a sense of purpose. How would your life be different?

3. Align your daily activities with your life's purpose.

4. Discover who you really are—in Christ.

5. Recognize that recovery is a journey.

6. Evaluate your motives. What are you really trying to accomplish?

7. Instead of waiting until you are a miserable, suicidal mess, cry out to God now so you can begin healing and living according to His plan for your life now.

8. Instead of roaming the house of your life aimlessly and wrestling monsters, surrender your struggles to God and accept His love, grace, and redemption into your life.

9. Join The Kingsman Academy now and surround yourself with the love, support, and kinship of Christian friends and mentors.

10. Build relationships with others to strengthen your relationship with God.

11. Acknowledge any "father wounds" you have been carrying around since childhood. Turn them over to God to begin healing immediately.

12. Recognize that, even if you had a good relationship with your earthly father, it can never come close to the love, protection, guidance, and mercy you will receive from your Heavenly Father.

13. Forgive yourself for your past sins and shortcomings, and

recognize that your past or present circumstances do not define who you are. You are a perfect child of God, created in His image. He loves you unconditionally.

14. Understand that as you become a believer and begin walking in the path God has planned for your life, you will experience growing pains. Sometimes you will feel frustration, but your Heavenly Father and fellow believers will support you during the growth process.

15. Stop trying to earn God's love. Jesus paid the ultimate price for our sins when He died on the cross. Just accept this Divine Gift and commit yourself to living within His will.

16. Expect significant changes in your attitude, views, and mood once you become redeemed, or saved from sin. It will improve every aspect of your life. Join the adventure!

17. Read the Bible, pray, and engage in fellowship with a fellow Kingsman so that you can get to know God more intimately. We must know God to know ourselves.

18. Accept God's love, and begin to heal.

19. Accept responsibility for your actions and attitude to grow and become a better version of yourself, which will honor God.

20. Focus on your God-ordained destiny.

21. Refuse to let your past control you or hold you back from the phenomenal success and happiness God wants you to have.

22. Don't start over; just start again—on the right path.

23. Lose the victim mentality; picture yourself as a victor instead of a victim.

24. Teach your children to be victors.

25. Discover and live your true (God-given) purpose.

26. Step out into the unknown by faith.

27. Make wise choices consciously.

28. Consider fasting to renew your physical strength.

29. Recognize your value.

30. Take good care of your body. It is God's temple.

31. There is no such thing as trying; just do it.

32. Identify the problem, and choose to fix it.

33. Make long-term changes in your attitude and lifestyle.

34. Let your uniqueness inspire you.

35. Nurture your relationships with others; they are vital to your well-being.

36. Find a mentor to help you grow.

37. Be a mentor to someone else, when you are ready.

38. Forgive those who have hurt you, even if—especially if—they don't deserve it. It isn't easy, but God expects us to forgive others if He is to forgive us. Forgiveness is the ultimate freedom.

39. Face your dangerous tendencies—the ones that put your relationships with your loved ones and God at risk.

40. Release all bitterness, and replace it with love and forgiveness.

41. Cherish your family.

42. Turn your hardships into lessons learned, both for yourself and others.

43. Dream huge dreams.

44. Know where you are and where you are going.

45. Know your God-given purpose; it is the foundation of the Kingsman Journey.

46. Strengthen your financial future by investing in income-producing real estate.

47. Understand how to use debt wisely to free up your cash for revenue-producing investments.

48. Be a good steward of your money to honor God and your family.

49. Begin with the end in mind. Know what your financial and life goals are first, and then work to achieve them.

50. Be clear about what you want in life.

51. Know your current financial position.

52. Keep more of what you earn.

53. Use leverage to optimize your financial well-being.

54. Be still, and listen for God's voice.

55. Strive for balance in your life; don't let work consume you.

56. Seek to fulfill your purpose, not just to make money. Success without fulfillment is the ultimate failure.

57. Other people can resent your success and try to destroy what you've built out of jealousy. If this happens, turn it over to God, and forgive them. But don't stop striving to honor God with your success.

58. Try to find the lesson God wants to teach you through difficult times.

59. Rely on God to provide you with strength when you feel weak and burdened.

60. When tempted to sin, pray to God and resist the urge. Giving in to sin creates an appetite for more sin, which can destroy your life, reputation, and relationships.

61. Recognize that when you sin, it becomes more difficult to satisfy your appetite for the things you should walk away from.

62. To heal, you must surrender your problem or addiction to God and detox.

63. Rely on God and a fellow friend to help you heal.

64. Acknowledge that you are a product of your environment and that the guidance you received as a child doesn't necessarily align with God's plan for you.

65. Be aware of issues that are keeping you from living the life God intended for you.

66. "Rewrite the script" to move forward, as necessary, replacing lessons you learned long ago with the truth of God's Word.

67. Show your emotions, even though you have probably always been taught that you shouldn't do so.

68. Know that being aware of an issue or problem is the first step in resolving it and healing from it.

69. Always continue learning, growing, and improving.

70. Live intentionally, making sure that every action you take and every word you speak aligns with your God-given purpose.

71. Be grateful for everything, even your hardships, because they are molding you into the person of character God wants you to be.

72. Live by design, not by default.

73. Abide by God's timing.

74. Design your life to control your own time.

75. Spend every moment wisely.

76. Be willing to listen and follow His call for your life.

77. Decide to change and to follow your dreams.

78. Keep in mind that time is the only thing you cannot get back, so cherish every moment as if it were your last.

79. Ask for direction on how you should be spending every minute of your day.

80. Have good strategies in place so life doesn't just sneak up on you.

81. Be intentional about every part of your day.

82. Don't allow people to pull you into their agendas.

83. Follow an effective strategy to live according to God's plan.

84. Picture your life as a blank canvas on which you can design it however you like. Define what every aspect of your ideal life looks like.

85. Let that vision reveal your God-given purpose.

86. Let your imagination run wild.

87. Surrender your life to God's design.

88. Lead by example.

89. Live your life by design, not by default, and work on achieving your optimum use of the quests in this book: purpose, spirit, soul, body, relationships, family, wealth, contribution, growth, fun, time, and dreams.

THE NEW YOU

Thank you so much for joining me in the *Kingsman* adventure. Though this is the book's conclusion, I want you to understand that these final pages are not the end, but a new beginning. A new beginning for a voyage toward a captivating destiny. A fresh start for an expedition that not only changes your own spirit, soul, and body, but one that will bring change to the world around you.

Along this journey, I have shared with you my stories, my dreams, and my lessons. I've revealed to you my purpose and my destiny. Why? Why would I share the most painful parts of my life with you? Why would I expose my weaknesses like that?

The reason I do this is because of what this story has done to me. God has so drastically changed me, I could not keep it to myself. My endurance of the many trials has allowed God to purify me and make me whole. But for this entire journey I have been on to be meaningful, the powerful transformation I experienced must be shared—I cannot keep it to myself.

> *So be truly glad. There is wonderful joy ahead, even though you must endure many trials for a little while. These trials will show that your faith is genuine. It is being tested as fire tests and purifies gold—though your faith is far more precious than mere gold. So when your faith remains strong through many trials, it will bring you much praise and glory and honor on the day when Jesus Christ is revealed to the whole world (1 Peter 1:6–7).*

I also shared my story with you because of what this has done for my family. My wife and sons now have hope for a better future. Our relatives and friends join us in rejoicing at the wonder of our God. Instead of being controlled by pains from the past, we are all relishing the privilege it has been to go on this journey, finding grace in every quest we encounter. I listen to my wife and hear the strength of her testimony. I listen to our children and smile at their wisdom. My three-year-old hugs me and says, "Daddy, you are awesome." What does that do to me? "I am a winner, and my brother is a winner, and my mommy is a winner, and you are a winner." What does that do to me when he says that? I cannot help but get excited about where God has brought us. Wonder has occurred; I cannot keep it to myself. We are not a family that is just another statistic of giving up. We are a family on the quest of grace—together.

And I offer you these stories because I see hope in you. You were created in God's image. You are invited to the Kingsman adventure. Through every quest, your life can grow and develop into Christlikeness.

You are being cultivated by your Creator. He wants you to begin The Journey of a Kingsman—learning your purpose, caring for yourself, joining the adventure with those who will mentor you, leaving a legacy,

> # HE WANTS YOU TO BEGIN THE JOURNEY OF A KINGSMAN

making major contributions, grasping the truth about Him, investing wisely, managing time, pursuing your dreams, and enjoying the process.

Before we finish, take a moment to glance into the mirror. We are not clones. Each one of us is unique. But we all crave an adventure, and these quests offer wonderful portions of this journey. See that purpose glancing back through the reflection as someone called by God to change the world.

That is what the Scriptures mean when God told him, "I have made you the

father of many nations." This happened because Abraham believed in the God who brings the dead back to life and who creates new things out of nothing (Rom. 4:17).

Keep on asking, and you will receive what you ask for. Keep on seeking, and you will find. Keep on knocking, and the door will be opened to you (Matt. 7:7).

Yes, I am thankful for what writing this has done in my life. Yes, I am thrilled at what experiencing this has provided for my family. It moves me in an amazing way and makes my heart smile as I think about what this can do for you. You are no longer the person you were. You are new. Today, you are new. And your future will be so much better than it would have been if you had not chosen to view yourself correctly and let yourself be guided in a mighty way by your Creator Himself.

Maybe you believe that but deep down still question how to find your unique role in this journey called life. I want you to always remember what I have shared with you throughout this book: I am where I am today because I decided to follow His voice. I am wired to do certain unique things that you are not. You are wired to do certain things that I am not. Look at your fingerprint—you are unique in every single way. There's no one in the whole world like you. Author Frederick Buechner gives a definition of "vocation" that can help us grasp how to find our own place in this world as we go through the Kingsman's journey and conquer the twelve quests of life:

> By and large, a good rule for finding out is this. The kind of work God usually calls you to is the kind of work (a) that you need most to do and (b) that the world most needs to have done. If you really get a kick out of your work, you've presumably met requirement (a) but if your work is writing TV deodorant commercials, the chances are you've missed requirement (b). On the other hand, if your work is being a doctor in a leper colony, you have probably met requirement (b), but most of the time you're bored and depressed by it, the chances

are you have not only bypassed (a) but probably aren't helping your patients much either. The place God calls you to is the place where your deep gladness and the world's deep hunger meet.[2]

Where is your place in this adventure? It must begin right where you are—releasing pains from the past that have often controlled you and defeating fears of the future that have often kept you from stepping forward. Right where you are—with your own gifts and personality, with your own wounds and scars, with your own story—begin the Kingsman Journey.

What will your story be when you finally share it with others?

Like that widow in 2 Kings 4, prepare the jars so the oil can be poured. The seeds have been sown into fertile ground. The days of being deaf, dumb, and blind are over. Pick a beautiful place in a tall building downtown and begin your own "coffee with friends" on Monday mornings at 7:00 a.m. Develop an environment where the voices that need to speak can be heard and the stories that ears need to hear can be heard so the soul has an opportunity to heal itself.

Find your purpose. Become a master in your area of expertise. No longer allow your past to control you.

Do not try to control all that God is doing. My initial thoughts of business changed because God turned my story into a better story. My original thoughts on this book changed because God guided it into a greater adventure than I could have ever created, had I depended on my own strength.

As I mentioned in the beginning, I'm not a travel agent sending you to a destination I've never been before. I am just your guide as a fellow traveler. A guide, as someone who has already been there and is now taking others with him. I am still enjoying each quest. It is, after all, a lifelong journey. A journey that I welcome you on and dare you to

---

2. Frederick Buechner, Author of *Wishful Thinking: A Theological ABC* (New York: Harper & Row, 1973), 118–19.

embark on. I hope to be able to keep guiding you along the way, if you'll let me.

Think again about the names I've written in this book, remembering that God used them to help shape my story just as my words are helping craft yours. Larry, Daniel, Tony, Robert, Rick—where would I be if I had not welcomed them into my quest? I wrote about them intentionally because I know the value of mentorship. I know how much being part of a healthy community of like-minded individuals can have in someone's life. And, although I was never a part of a community that I could plug into daily and I had to face most of the challenges along the way on my own, I am thankful to have developed a community where you can plug in and not have to go through this on your own.

As I mentioned before, a good way to learn is through your own mistakes. A great and effective way to learn, however, is through some else's mistakes. You now have a chance to be mentored by someone who has already been there and is willing to help guide you along the way. And, depending what season of life you are currently in, you might be ready to mentor someone else.

Continue the conversation on this journey. No matter how far we are geographically separated, join the dialogue, and let's travel together. *The Kingsman Academy* invites you to travel in community—you are no longer alone.

You bring with you struggles from the past. Let's face them together and let God bring deliverance. You entered this journey with worries about the future. Let's defeat the giants through His power. You will have questions—ask them. You will have fears—let us help you fight through them. You will want to quit—refuse to give up; this is only the beginning. You will sense occasional attractions to take dangerous turns—resist the lures, and let us bring accountability into your life.

Where are you today? Where do you hope to be next week, next month, next year? Where do you desire to be a decade from today?

You won't be able to reach the destination by a simple stroke of luck. Your spirit will guide you there. Even when life throws unexpected surprises your way, you will be able to make wise choices. Choose the right path. Choose to travel the path of a *Kingsman.*

Good days and years await you, my friend. Adventures of grace are ahead. Do not miss them. Do not miss this moment. Always remember: Life happens *for* you, not *to* you.

Now is *the* time.
Now is *your* time.
Now is *our* time.
I look forward to having you as part of our community.

Blessings,
Diogo

Now may the God of peace make you holy in every way, and may your whole spirit and soul and body be kept blameless until our Lord Jesus Christ comes again. God will make this happen, for he who calls you is faithful (1 Thess. 5:23–24).

Diogo Esteves is the founder and president of The Kingsman Academy (TKA), a worldwide movement that was created to equip people in the twelve essential elements of life while empowering them to become financially free so they can focus their time on fulfilling their God-given calling and live lives of meaning, significance, and joy on the way to their ultimate destiny.

Prior to founding TKA, Diogo spent most of his time working in the fields of insurance, investments, mortgage, and real estate, where he built a multimillion-dollar business.

He was born in Brazil and moved to the United States at age seventeen. He achieved significant financial success before the age of thirty. Yet, despite his outward financial success, being happily married to his wife, Daniela, having two wonderful sons, Matthew and Lucca, and living an overall life that most men only dream of, Diogo often found himself battling deep depression and sexual addiction. Because a cloud so dark hung over his life, he spent most of his time researching ways to commit suicide and doing things that would ultimately lead him down a path of destruction.

Throughout his own journey, Diogo has discovered secrets that enabled him to move past his biggest challenges and develop a powerful and clear sense of direction never before experienced. His life is now dedicated to helping others who have decided to set out on a journey of self-discovery to help them achieve their full potential and their wildest goals and dreams in life.

ABOUT THE AUTHOR

NOTES

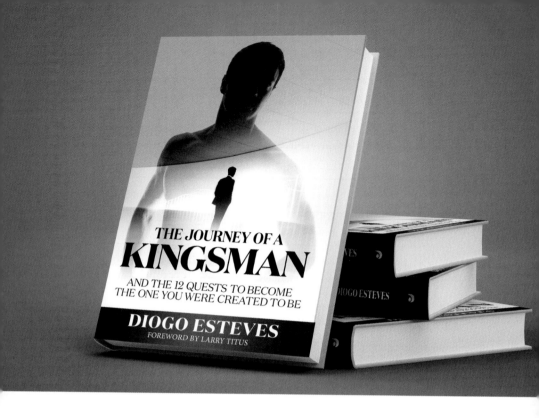

ARE YOU READY TO BECOME A KINGSMAN?

My hope is that reading *The Journey of a Kingsman: And the 12 Quests to Become the One You Were Created to Be* has sparked within you a hunger, a longing to step into a larger destiny and to embrace a bigger dream, vision, and plan for your life.

This book isn't a magical pill meant to solve all your problems. However, your life is a journey. My only goal is to equip you to go through this journey with an amazing sense of purpose, a great desire to impact the world, and the understanding that God created you to be and do so much more than what you are experiencing right now.

This is why The Kingsman Academy was born. I wanted to establish a community of like minded individuals with a shared vision, mission, and purpose to live their lives by the highest possible standards and, as a result, positively influence those around them in a major way, while achieving a great amount of success in every area of their lives.

Please don't think that joining me and others on this journey is about being perfect. God knows we are all flawed, broken, and, candidly, messed up. We all get beaten up and sometimes even knocked down, but I have news for you: you don't have to stay down! By supporting one another on our respective life journeys as we all discover and follow God's plan for our lives, we can achieve more than we ever dreamed.

SO HERE IS MY UNIQUE INVITATION TO YOU:

Take the leap, and join our community. There's no test to take or anything to prove. Just say, "I'm in" by downloading our "Kingsman" App in the Google play and Apple store or by visiting

www.thekingsmanacademy.com/apply

Embrace change. Royalty awaits you. I will see you soon.

Follow The Kingsman Academy

/thekingsmanacademy

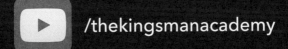

/thekingsmanacademy

/thekingsmanacademy